LEGENDARY SNEAKERS

LEGENDARY SNEAKERS

A Curated Guide to 200 Iconic Kicks

Record Breakers • Stars of Pop Culture • Themed Designs • Collabs

Tonton Gibs

SCHIFFER PUBLISHING

4880 Lower Valley Road • Atglen, PA 19310

Other Schiffer Books on Related Subjects:

The Sneaker Book: 50 Years of Sports Shoe Design by Tina Skinner and Melissa Cardona, 978-0-7643-2188-7

How to Customize Kicks: Step-by-Step Instructions and Inspiration from the Sneaker Experts by Customize Kicks Magazine, 978-0-7643-6553-9

Originally published as *Sneakers: Incroyables Records*, © 2023, Éditions Larousse, Paris
Translated from the French by Liza Tripp

Library of Congress Control Number: 2025930648

Cover design by Jack Chappell
Production design by Kate North
Type set in Anton/DIN Pro Bold/DIN Pro Regular

ISBN: 978-0-7643-7025-0

ePub: 978-1-5073-0610-9

Printed in China

10 9 8 7 6 5 4 3 2 1

FSC
www.fsc.org
MIX
Paper | Supporting responsible forestry
FSC® C167893

Published by Schiffer Publishing, Ltd.

4880 Lower Valley Road

Atglen, PA 19310

Phone: (610) 593-1777; Fax: (610) 593-2002

Email: info@schifferbooks.com

Web: www.schifferbooks.com

For our complete selection of fine books on this and related subjects, please visit our website at www.schifferbooks.com. You may also write for a free catalog.

Schiffer Publishing's titles are available at special discounts for bulk purchases for sales promotions or premiums. Special editions, including personalized covers, corporate imprints, and excerpts, can be created in large quantities for special needs. For more information, contact the publisher.

CONTENTS

or those of you who don't already know me, I'm Tonton Gibs—streetwear enthusiast and lover of gleaming shoes. You're holding in your hands my third opus. When people find out my story, they think it's amazing that I've been able to assemble these beautiful books on such incredible topics. I have Larousse to thank for trusting me with these projects. After *Cultissimes Sneakers* (*Cult Classic Sneakers*), which was a huge success thanks to its many readers, I collaborated with Uncle Texaco and Teki Latex on *Street Style*, a wonderful book that traced the evolution of streetwear from the 1980s to the present—I'm especially proud of that book, which you can now find in every fashion school's library. And now here's a new masterpiece on the world of sneakers, this time with a unique angle.

I hope you enjoy this lovely book. You'll learn about incredible records, although it's been hard to get precise numbers from brands, given how frenetic the sneaker industry has become. You'll also discover several iconic pairs and lastly, some of my personal favorites.

Get ready to uncover the highest-selling pair in the world, the most expensive pair in the world, the sneakers that made headlines on Valentine's Day or Halloween—and even the pairs that have lit up the big screen!

RECORD-BREAKING SNEAKERS

THE OLDEST SNEAKERS IN THE WORLD!

WHERE DID SNEAKERS COME FROM?

Where Does the Word "Sneaker" Come From?

The word "sneaker" comes from the English verb "to sneak," meaning "to slip in and out, to creep in surreptitiously." The expression was first used in 1862 by women in a prison in Brixton, England, to refer to the night officers' shoes. These pairs, which they found to be "sneaky," were not sneakers in the strict sense of the word, but simply rubber-soled shoes.

Incidentally, we do know that the word "sneakers" was used in 1887, because an article about tennis in the *Boston Journal* remarked that the players referred to their tennis shoes as "sneakers."

The Rubber-Soled Shoes of Basketball Players

The long history of basketball shoes began in 1895 in the United States, with the term "rubber-soled shoe." The model gave its name to the first official pair created for basketball games. The shoe was produced in 1904 by the Spalding company (now more well known for its balls): the rubber-soled "Expert" Basket Ball Shoe.

Note that the onomatopoeia "sneak-sneak," which mimics the noise that sneakers make on the floors of basketball courts, also has the same origin.

The First True Sneakers

Keds were the first pair of shoes to officially be called "sneakers." The United States Rubber Company, a rubber and tire company, created the shoe in 1916. As a sidenote, recall that the name "Keds" is a contraction of "peds" (from *pedis*, "foot" in Latin) and the English word "kids."

THE SPALDING "EXPERT" BASKET BALL SHOE

THIS shoe is designed for expert use only. It is equipped with a pure gum rubber sole, very expensive and not particularly durable, but really the only material that has sufficient "abrasive" quality to grip the floor and not slide, even on a waxed surface. Furthermore, we make the sole with our special "diamond point" surface, something

Showing Sole with Diamond Point

never attempted before, and we claim that in this combination of "diamond point" surface and pure gum rubber sole we have solved the problem that has baffled both ourselves and every other shoe manufacturer until now. We present the No. BBR Spalding Expert Basket Ball Shoe as the only perfect basket ball shoe ever made for expert use.

We do not guarantee the soles of these shoes.

No. BBR. Spalding "EXPERT" Shoe. Pair, **$8.00**

Prices subject to change without notice
Send for handsomely illustrated catalogue of all athletic sports

Communications addressed to
A. C. SPALDING & BROS.
in any of the following cities will receive attention:
For street numbers see inside front cover of this book.

Montreal, Canada					London, England
New York	Boston	Philadelphia	Chicago	St. Louis	San Francisco
Buffalo	Pittsburg	Washington	Cleveland	Cincinnati	Denver
Syracuse	Baltimore	New Orleans	Detroit	Kansas City	Minneapolis

These prices in effect July 5, 1907.

The Keds "Champion" was a canvas shoe with a slightly thicker rubber sole. The casual model was frequently worn by tennis players in a high-top version (and later a low-top one). You can find the same shoe to this day, albeit in a plainer form.

In 1917, or barely a year after Keds were created, a company owned by Marquis Mills called the Converse Rubber Shoe Company—still today known as Converse—launched production of the first pair of basketball shoes: the Converse All Star, which would become known as the Converse "Chuck Taylor" All Star.

It was not until 1949 that the Keds brand launched Pro-Keds, which offered basketball shoes.

Therefore, Keds, Pro-Keds, and, above all, Converse dominated the dedicated basketball sneaker market for the first half of the twentieth century.

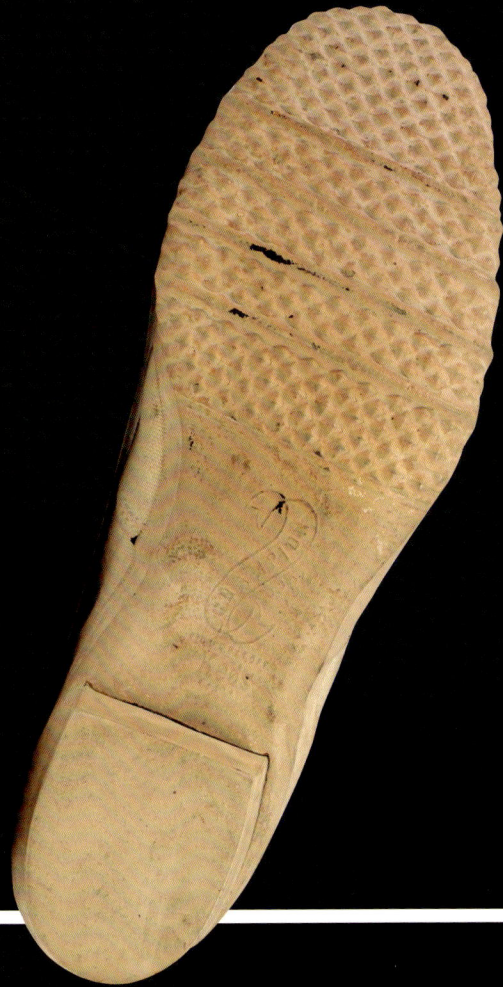

RECORD-SETTING SALES

Three Behemoths

So then, was it Adidas, Converse, or Nike that made the all-time best-selling sneaker in the world?

Although Nike is the youngest brand (the company was established in 1971, while Converse was founded in 1908 and Adidas in 1949), it is nevertheless the market leader. Indeed, the American giant sells the most sneakers to this day, boasting iconic models such as the AF1s, AM1s, and Jordans.

What Is the Most Purchased Model in the World, of All the Brands?

It's hard to answer this question (although it's something everyone wonders about), because the majority of the big sneaker brands are reluctant to communicate their sales figures. Nevertheless, two models seem to stand out: the Stan Smith Adidas Originals and the Converse All Star Chuck Taylor 1970s.

Stan Smith Adidas Originals

In 1990, the Stan Smith Adidas Originals entered the *Guiness World Records* as the all-time best-selling shoe in the world, with twenty-two million pairs sold.

In late 2011, Adidas stopped producing this iconic model, which over time created frustration—and therefore demand—among many of the shoe's fans. Once production resumed, sales went completely through the roof, reaching the astronomical number of seventy million pairs sold! Today, the brand no longer discloses its sales figures.

Adidas wanted to play a crucial role in finding solutions to combat plastics pollution, and in January 2021 it reworked its iconic Stan Smith model to be eco-friendly. The shoe now has a white Primegreen upper and is manufactured using high-performance recycled materials, such as outsoles made out of white recycled rubber and an experimental canvas.

Note that while the Stan Smith is certainly an undeniable classic, it is nonetheless not the most fashionable shoe of our times, because the sneaker world has really changed and evolved in recent years. Recall that other pairs have set off sneaker crazes—such as the Air Force 1 in the late nineties and early aughts, and even the Adidas Yeezy (before the famous brand had its falling out with Kanye West . . .). Today, sales of the legendary Jordans are again blowing up at Nike. You can truly take nothing for granted in the sneaker world!

Converse All Star Chuck Taylor 1970 High-Top

When we think of sales records, one iconic pair stands out: the Converse All Star Chuck Taylor 1970. It's true that this is one of the oldest pairs in the world, which gives it a nice lead in terms of sales. This model has been made in thousands of colors, which have been further interpreted with many incredibly varied materials. The brand has also made many different style updates, and it has teamed up with major artists and fashion houses.

By 2013, Converse had sold more than eight hundred million pairs of its various models. And it is quite probable that the large majority of these shoes were All Star Chuck Taylors, because—even though sneakers were not the fashion phenomenon they are currently—the All Star Chuck Taylor was already a basketball world icon. This pair moreover perfectly illustrates the definition of the word "mainstream" in the sense of "being of the masses," since it traveled from the street to the rock world, and then over to the punk movement of the 1970s. People have always liked its timeless lines. In fact, the All Star Chuck Taylors were later renamed the "Chuck Taylor 70," in homage to that era.

While it may be hard to confirm that any one pair is sold more than another, due to the secret culture surrounding the sneaker market as a whole, it seems pretty safe to say that the Converse All Star Chuck Taylor 70 has been the top-selling pair of sneakers in the world since it was created in 1917.

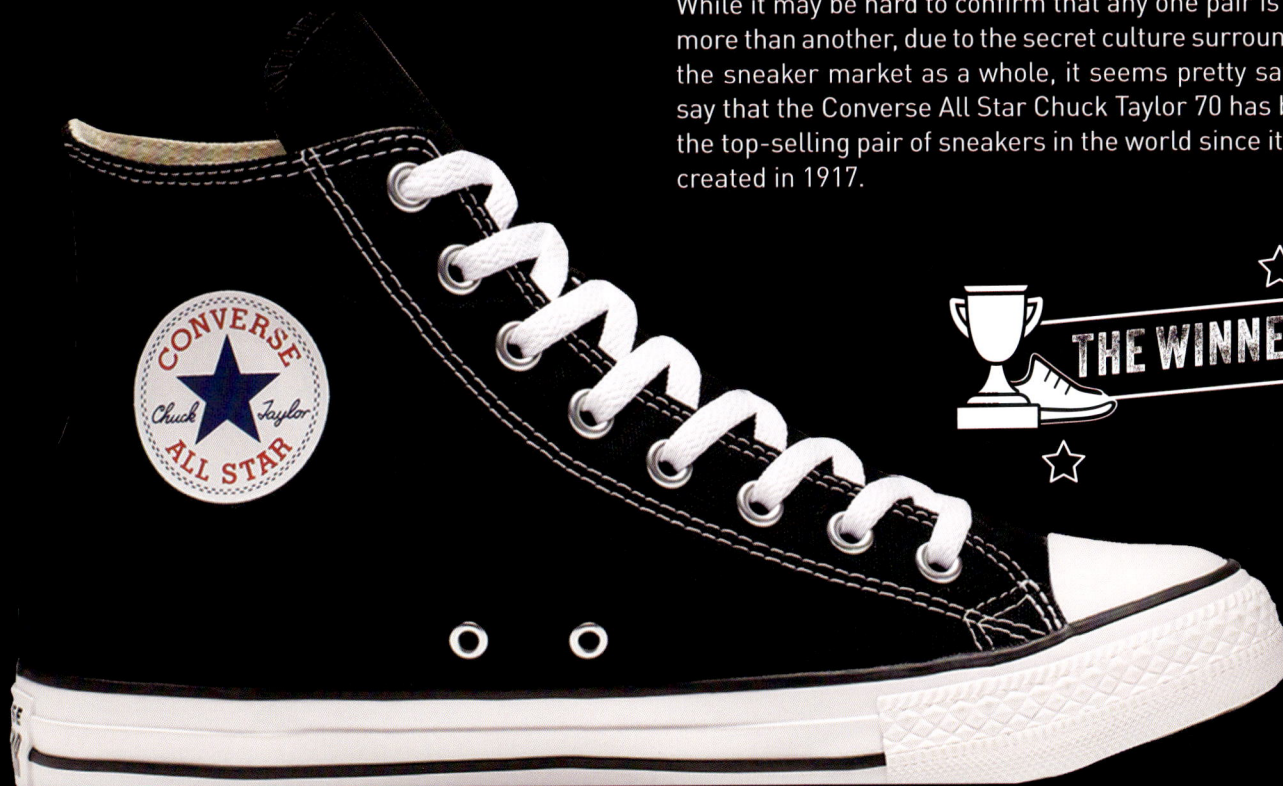

THE WINNER

GOLDEN SNEAKERS!

THE MOST EXPENSIVE PAIRS THROUGHOUT HISTORY

So you thought only works of art were sold at auction? Well, sneakers are too!

Air Jordan XIII OG "Bred" 1998: $2,200,000

On April 11, 2023, the Sotheby's auction house shattered the sales records for a pair of sneakers: the Air Jordan XIII OG "Bred" (Black and Red), which were worn and signed by Michael Jordan, sold at $2,200,000. I must admit that this incredible pair is legendary because the iconic athlete wore them during his last NBA Finals against the Utah Jazz. With the victory, Michael Jordan secured his second three-peat of the NBA title, winning him his sixth NBA championship overall.

THE WINNER

Prior to the second game of the series, a ball boy who was at practice the night before had found Michael Jordan's jacket and brought it back to him; in return, the player had offered to give the boy his sneakers after Game 2. After the game, Michael Jordan took off his shoes in the locker room and signed them. This is the only pair of basketball shoes Michael Jordan wore during an NBA Finals game that has been authenticated by the MeiGray Group, the official authenticator of the NBA. This pair has thus been dubbed "The Last Dance" because Michael Jordan wore them during his last NBA Finals with the Bulls—hence its importance! With the hammer coming down at more than $2 million, these Jordan 13s unquestionably became the most expensive pair in the world . . . at least at the time.

Nike Air Yeezy 1 "Grammy Worn": $1,800,000

Before the Jordan 13s in 2023, the previous record was held by the Nike Air Yeezy 1 "Grammy Worn," once again sold by Sotheby's, a leading authority for art and luxury auction sales.

After having signed a contract with Nike in 2007, Kanye West worked on several prototypes with Tinker Hatfield

In 2015, as part of the launch of the Heat Check website founded by Justin Ashby, the pair was put up for auction at a reserve price of $75,000.

Six years later, in 2021, the "Grammy" Yeezy again shattered all of Sotheby's records, reaching the astronomical price of $1.8 million. Only time will tell whether it was a sound

Nike Air Ship White Red 1984: $1,472,000

This is a pair that Michael Jordan wore during his first season with the Chicago Bulls and is signed by the athlete. It was put up for auction at Sotheby's on October 24, 2021, shortly after the auctioning of the "Grammy" Yeezys. Michael Jordan had signed and given the pair to seller Tommie Tim III Lewis, who'd been a ball boy for the Denver Nuggets during the 1984–85 season.

Sold at Christie's auction house in August 2020, this pair was worn by Michael Jordan on August 25, 1985, in a friendly match against JuveCaserta in Trieste, Italy, during a promotional tour organized by Nike. The highlight of this match was a legendary slam dunk by the "Black Cat" that broke the Plexiglas of the backboard. During the auction,

Christie's also highlighted the fact that there was still a piece of Plexiglas under the sole of the left shoe.

For your information, the shoes worn by Michael Jordan are often two different sizes, US 13 (left foot) and US 13.5 (right foot), because one of his feet is larger than the other.

Air Jordan 1 OG "Chicago" (Player Sample): $560,000

In May 2020—three months before the Jordan 1 record at Christie's—a "player sample" (a shoe reserved for a player) that Michael Jordan had worn and signed in 1985 was sold for $560,000 at Sotheby's.

Sotheby's notes that the code inside the shoes says "850204 TYPS." 850204 refers to the production date: These shoes

were manufactured in 1985, between February (02) and April (04). TYPS means "Tong Yang Player Sample," which indicates that the shoes are player samples produced by the Tong Yang factory. These shoes came with a letter of authentication from PSA/DNA and an opinion letter from MEARS Authentication, LLC, which declares that the pair is authentic.

Nike Waffle Racing Flat "Moon Shoe" 1972: $437,500

Sotheby's and Stadium Goods sold this pair in July 2019. There are only twelve pairs of this model in the world, and this pair seems to be the only one that was never worn. The shoes were purchased by Miles Nadal, a Canadian entrepreneur and collector, to be displayed in his personal museum in Toronto.

This pair, destined for the track, has a particularly interesting history. The model was actually designed by Bill Bowerman, cofounder of Nike, with Phil Knight. At the time, Bill Bowerman was very involved in designing sneakers for American athletes in preparation of the Olympic selections.

There was no shortage of quirkiness involved in designing a model with true traction and good cushioning, with Bowerman even conducting one of the first tests on the design of this pair by melting down rubber in his wife's waffle iron—hence the name "Nike Waffle." The outsole is divided into two parts, because, at that time, Nike did not yet have the technology needed to produce a sole in a single piece. The nickname "Moon Shoe" refers to the waffled patterns of the sole, which leave imprints similar to the ones astronauts Neil Armstrong and Edwin "Buzz" Aldrin left on the moon in 1969.

Air Jordan 1 OG "Chicago" 1984: $420,000

This pair worn by Michael Jordan (who signed both shoes) was sold in June 2021 by Grey Flannel Auctions, a leader in auction sales of sports items in the United States. The player had given this pair to his favorite photographer, Robert Crawford, following a game between the Bulls and the Pacers on March 26, 1985.

Note that it's becoming increasingly common for sneakers to reach this price range nowadays.

Grey Flannel Auctions Jordan 1 Converse Fastbreak Mid: $190,373

SCP Auctions sold these sneakers in June 2017. Michael Jordan wore this pair of Converse Fastbreak Mids (which he signed) at the 1984 Los Angeles Olympics. They were picked up by a ball boy and are now considered to be the last pair of sneakers that Michael Jordan wore as an amateur.

The photo above shows the pair of Converse Fastbreak Mids on display before an auction at Sotheby's New York on July 7, 2021.

Focus on the "Four-Minute-Mile Shoe"

Here's another noteworthy record, even if it's a bit removed from the world of sneakers. On May 6, 1954, Roger Bannister became the first athlete to run a mile in less than four minutes (3 minutes, 59 seconds). This record lasted only six weeks, but it nevertheless remains an important step in running history. On that day, the runner was wearing a handcrafted pair in black leather, which was later sold at auction in London for £266,500 (then approximately $408,545) in September 2015. This pair is known as the "four-minute-mile shoes."

Air Jordan XII "Flu Game" (1997): $104,765

Sold by Grey Flannel Auctions in December 2013, this pair is definitely the most popular Jordan XII—its link to a legendary sports moment makes the shoes exceptional!

On June 11, 1997, the night before Game 5 of the NBA Finals, Michael Jordan got food poisoning from a bad pizza. His team even suspected that someone intentionally tried to poison him, given the importance of the upcoming game. Still, Jordan showed up on the court the next day, despite the fact that he was feeling terrible. The press quickly reported that he'd gotten the flu. He nevertheless managed to score 38 points and lead his team to a 90–88 victory. This classic game, along with the pair of sneakers Michael Jordan wore in it, have since been coined the "Flu Game," although it was later confirmed that he'd definitely had food poisoning.

After the game, Michael Jordan signed his sneakers and gave them to a young Preston Truman, then a ball boy. Why? Preston had dropped off applesauce and cookies in front of Jordan's locker after having heard him say he loved those foods. The player was so touched by this thoughtful gesture that he spontaneously signed his pair of sneakers and gave them to the young ball boy from the Utah Jazz. Fifteen years later, Preston Truman decided to sell these sneakers at auction with an opening bid of $5,000; the pair sold at $104,765.

The photo below shows the Air Jordan 12 model that became famous.

SOLD !

Here's a list of some of the pairs that have been sold at auction at dizzyingly high prices. Happily, all the proceeds from these sales (which were organized by major brands) went to charities.

Let's begin with a unique item sold by Sotheby's in December 2020, which is a true work of art. This pair is actually the result of a 100 percent German collaboration between Adidas and Meissen, a company known worldwide for its high-quality, delicately crafted porcelain. This premium leather model was hand painted by Meissen craftsmen, with 950 grams of authentic porcelain superimposed onto it. It took six months and several round trips between the Adidas factory in Herzogenaurach and the Meissen factory (in the city of Meissen) to make one pair.

This incredible model is a mash-up of two icons: the Adidas ZX8000 and the famous Krater de Meissen vase, which was designed in 1856. The pair, which was painted by four artisans from three different Meissen departments, incorporates fifteen of the Meissen vase's 130 patterns. Sotheby's had estimated this rare pair to be worth close to $1 million, and it was ultimately sold at auction for $126,000. The entire amount went to the Brooklyn Museum.

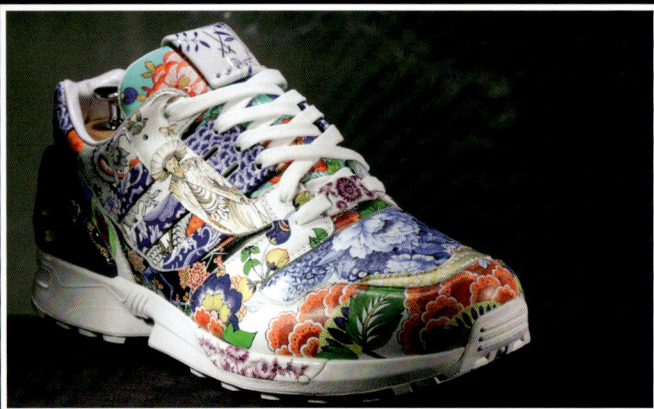

Adidas × Meissen ZX8000 Porcelain

Release date: 12/16/2020
Sale price: $126,000 (size US 9)

Futura Laboratories × Virgil Abloh × Nike Dunk Low "Virgil Abloh"

Release date: 04/14/2023
Auction: estimated as between $2,000 and $4,000
Results of sale:
UNC model, size US 5: $25,400
Syracuse model, size US 6: $57,150
UNC model, size US 7: $76,200
Syracuse model, size US 8: $76,200
UNC model, size US 9: $76,200
Syracuse model, size US 10: $107,950
UNC model, size US 11: $82,550
Syracuse model, size US 12: $63,500
Total: $565,150

The Off-White show during the 2020 Paris Fashion Week (Spring–Summer Collection) was one of the last events that famous creative director Virgil Abloh attended before his death. It was during this event that the Nike Dunk Low FL made its first appearance. The sneakers generated an immediate buzz on social media sites, especially because Virgil Abloh and the New York graffiti artist Futura had done everything possible to prevent any information from being leaked before the show. On the catwalk, pairs of Nike Dunk Lows were on the feet of the models dressed in clothing from the Off-White × Futura collection, which featured pictures of cult personalities such as the Pointman.

It was Virgil Abloh's passion for streetwear that led him to direct this collaboration of the Off-White collection and these two pairs of timeless Dunks. He came up with two different shades: a blue pair in the colors of the University of North Carolina (UNC), where Michael Jordan earned his stripes, and an orange pair in the colors of Syracuse University.

Incidentally, note that the orange Nike Dunks have been known as the "Syracuse" since they were created—the late Peter Moore had designed the very first Dunks in 1985 for the "Nike College Colors," which then consisted of six pairs of Dunk Highs in the colors of West Coast universities and six others from the East Coast. The slogan of the pack, "Be true to your school," explains the Nike Dunks' nicknames, which often refer to the colors of the university teams. Yet, Futura chose the blue and orange shades of this model to pay homage to his favorite Major League Baseball team, the New York Mets. The pair is likewise a nod to New York skateboarder Danny Supa's debut 2002 collaboration, since the Nike SB Dunk Low used orange and blue in tribute to the New York Knicks basketball team. Both pairs have the initials "FL" engraved on the heel, referring to New York graffiti artist Futura's label, Futura Laboratories. These letters appeared for the first time on the Futura × Nike SB Dunk High "For Love or Money" in 2004.

Alas, the few pairs of Nike Dunk Low FLs that were produced for the 2020 Paris Fashion Week (Spring–Summer Collection) were all given to friends and family of the designers, while the public impatiently waited for the model to become available for purchase. Finally, just eight pairs were produced and sold at auction at Sotheby's, to benefit the Virgil Abloh Foundation and other charities supported by Futura, for a total price of $565,150.

Let's now return to the auctions benefiting the Michael J. Fox Foundation.

In 2011, 1,500 pairs of Nike Mags were sold in auctions Nike organized on eBay: They brought in $4,700,000.

In 2016, eighty-nine new pairs were sold, this time generating $6,950,000. One pair took in $200,000 at the foundation's charity gala, the highest price ever recorded for a Nike MAG!

Nike MAG

Release dates: 09/08/2011 and 10/04/2016
Sale at auction
Resale price (2011): $16,200–$32,400 (€15,000–€30,000) as of 2023
Resale price (2016): $43,200–$86,400 (€40,000–€80,000) as of 2023

In all, $11,650,000 was collected for the Michael J. Fox Foundation to finance research on Parkinson's disease.

Louis Vuitton × Nike Air Force 1 by Virgil Abloh

Release dates: from 01/26/22 to 02/09/22
Sale at auction: opening bid $2,000
Resale price: several hundred thousand dollars

THE WINNER

This pair, the result of a collaboration between French luxury brand Louis Vuitton and Nike, created quite the buzz upon its release. At the time, Louis Vuitton's creative director was none other than Virgil Abloh, who had brought the house to the height of its glory. Following Abloh's sudden death on November 28, 2021, you might have thought that the 2022 auction would have been canceled or postponed. Yet, the sale went on, and the funds were reinvested in the Virgil Abloh Post-Modern Scholarship Fund, an organization that seeks to promote equity and inclusion in the fashion industry by offering scholarships to African American students.

Virgil Abloh had already put his spin on the classics for several years, with Nike and his brand Off-White. The Louis Vuitton × Air Force 1 shoes were designed for the Louis Vuitton Spring–Summer 2022 menswear show. On that occasion, Abloh worked on one of the greatest classics of sneaker and hip-hop culture: the Nike Air Force 1. Abloh added the legendary monogram of the French fashion house to the original model designed by Bruce Kilgore in 1982. It was a revolution! It must be said that the famous designer Dapper Dan had already put the Louis Vuitton

monogram on the Nike Air Force 1's swoosh in 1988 for Rob Base and DJ E-Z Rock's album It Takes Two, although at the time it was considered more a bootleg or custom pair than an official collaboration.

Two hundred pairs handmade in Louis Vuitton's ateliers in Fiesso d'Artico in northern Italy were thus put up for auction at Sotheby's and exhibited in New York. Each pair was accompanied by a pilot Louis Vuitton case made out of monogrammed orange Taurillon leather, exclusively designed for the auction. The starting price was set at $2,000, and estimated sale prices were between $5,000 and $15,000 per pair. Following Abloh's' death and given the exclusivity of the model, the estimates were largely exceeded: The Air Force 1 × Louis Vuitton sneakers flew out at astronomical prices ranging from $75,000 to $352,800 per pair for the only size—US 5. In all, the sale brought in the record sum of $25 million!

In parallel to this sale, the designer's friends received F&F (Friends and Family) pairs announcing the release of a collection of nine Nike Air Force 1 High and Low models, which came out in June 2022.

MICHAEL JORDAN, KING OF SNEAKERS

THE MOST LUCRATIVE PARTNERSHIPS BETWEEN AN ATHLETE AND A BRAND

A Well-Conceived Career Move

Although *Forbes* magazine ranked him the 1,045th wealthiest person in the world in 2025, Michael Jordan topped Sportico's 2024 list of the highest-paid athletes of all time. At the time, the media outlet, which covers the business of sports, reported that Jordan had earned an estimated $3.7 billion adjusted for inflation.

Nonetheless, his career as a professional NBA player, as exceptional as it was, brought him "only" approximately $90 million! Did the famous basketball player demonstrate some keen business sense while awaiting his retirement from professional sports? Without a doubt, seeing as Michael Jordan is now co-owner of a NASCAR (23XI Racing) team and has invested in DraftKings and Dapper Labs, which are sports betting and blockchain businesses. Furthermore, his partnerships with companies such as Hanes and Gatorade are likewise very profitable. Yet, the bulk of his revenue comes from the Charlotte Hornets NBA team, which he owned from 2010 to 2023, along with (it goes without saying) his incredible and phenomenal contract with Nike!

Jordan Brand

Everyone knows the Jordan Brand's famous Jumpman logo, and the company, which has transcended eras and generations, is still a sound investment. Knowing that Michael Jordan gets 5 percent on every Jordan Brand–stamped item and considering that in 2022 the brand declared more than $5 billion in taxable income and other revenue, we can estimate that Michael Jordan earned around $250 million that year thanks to this brand alone—nearly $8 per second!

DID YOU KNOW ?

The famous Jumpman logo does not depict Michael Jordan making a slam dunk! In reality, this logo was inspired by a photo of the player doing a ballet move. During a shoot organized by Life magazine for the 1984 Olympics, Michael Jordan was photographed jumping in place, legs extended, a basketball in his left hand and Converses on his feet. One year later, when the athlete signed with Nike, the brand reproduced the pose during a shoot to promote the Air Jordan I sneakers.

Jordan Brand products were originally stamped with the Wings logo, designed by Peter Moore, which depicted a ball with wings. The designer supposedly came up with the idea on a plane, when the little boy seated next to him was given a pin with pilot wings on it. This strong symbol had seemed to perfectly fit Michael Jordan, a man who could "fly." In 1987, Tinker Hatfield designed the Jumpman logo, which he based on a Peter Moore sketch. In 1988 the Jumpman replaced the Wings logo on the Air Jordan IIIs and became the signature mark of all Jordan products.

SNEAKERS
ON THE
BIG SCREEN

NOW SHOWING

Nike and Jordan Brand

It's not surprising that it's still primarily Nike and Michael Jordan that dominate this cinephile section. Let's start by mentioning the Nike Air Command Forces that Woody Harrelson wore in *White Men Can't Jump* (1992). Fun fact: in the 2023 remake, Jack Harlow, who reprises the role, wears a pair of New Balance 650S. Maybe something to do with the change in era?

Pairs of Nike Jordans were used to create Batman's boots in at least two of the superhero films: Nike Air Trainer IIs were worn in *Batman* (1989), and Air Jordan VIs in *Batman Returns* (1992).

An Air Jordan 6 from *Batman*

I'll also mention the Nike Blazers worn in *Magic Baskets* (2002), the Nike Air More Uptempos worn in *George of the Jungle* (1997), the Nike Vandal High in *Terminator* (1984), and the Air Jordan XIIIs sported in *He Got Game* (1998). Let's conclude this nonexhaustive list of the ubiquitous Nikes worn on film by mentioning the comedies *Lottery Ticket* (2010), with Lil Bow Wow, or, more recently, *You People* (2023): Both were veritable odes to sneakers. This was also the case for *Kicks* (2016), but with a more dramatic setting, and in the film *Air* that came out in 2023, which retraces the start of the collaboration between Michael Jordan and Nike and the creation of the Air Jordan 1 shoe

He Got Game (1998)

George of the Jungle (1997)

Air (2023)

Krush Groove (1985)

Rocky IV (1985)

Adidas

Adidas features extensively in the film *Krush Groove* (1985), starring Russell Simmons and the group Run-DMC, among others. As a sidenote, Krush Groove was the first artist on historic hip-hop label Def Jam Recordings. I'll also mention the film *Rocky IV* (1985), in which Rocky Balboa is dressed exclusively in the three-stripe brand's apparel. Lastly, the films *Blade Runner* (1982), *Beverly Hills Cop* (1984), and *Home Alone* (1990) feature the Adidas Forum Lows.

New Balance

Let's now talk about New Balance and its role in a hilarious film starring Steve Carell and Ryan Gosling: *Crazy, Stupid, Love*. The Boston brand could have gone ballistic, considering how much the pair was mocked in this 2011 film, in which Cal Weaver (Steve Carell) undergoes a very aggressive makeover at the hands of Jacob Palmer (Ryan Gosling).

Right in the middle of a shopping mall, Ryan Gosling asks Steve Carell:

"What happened to your feet?"

"What do you mean? These are my 407s."

"Oh, they're 407s. Can I see them?"

"Yeah. These offer a lot of support," says Cal, taking them off and handing them over.

"Right," says Jacob, immediately tossing them over the railing alongside them.

"Woah! Come on!"

The NB 407s were a pair of well-priced, mainstream New Balances that you could find more or less everywhere in the United States for $50. A few years later, this type of model was coined "dad shoes," or even "ugly kicks." The pairs then became a cult favorite, and this scene of *Crazy, Stupid, Love* is now used as a reference for explaining the dad shoe fad.

He's been chased, thrown through a window, and arrested.
Eddie Murphy is a Detroit cop on vacation in Beverly Hills.

BEVERLY HILLS
cop

PARAMOUNT PICTURES PRESENTS A DON SIMPSON/JERRY BRUCKHEIMER PRODUCTION IN ASSOCIATION WITH EDDIE MURPHY PRODUCTIONS·A MARTIN BREST FILM
EDDIE MURPHY·BEVERLY HILLS COP·MUSIC BY HAROLD FALTERMEYER·SCREENPLAY BY DANIEL PETRIE, JR.·STORY BY DANILO BACH AND DANIEL PETRIE, JR.
PRODUCED BY DON SIMPSON AND JERRY BRUCKHEIMER·DIRECTED BY MARTIN BREST·MOTION PICTURE SOUNDTRACK ALBUM ON MCA RECORDS AND TAPES
A PARAMOUNT PICTURE

Reebok

In the case of Reebok, there are a few references to keep in mind, such as the film *Blue Chips* (1993) with Nick Nolte, who plays an impassioned coach training players such as Shaquille O'Neal and Penny Hardaway. The film shows players lacing up their Reebok Pump Verticals during the All-Star Games. Reebok also made a strong impact in *Aliens* (1986), with the design of the Reebok Alien Stomper, which you can see on the feet of Ellen Ripley, played by Sigourney Weaver.

Blue Chips (1993)

What About Vans?

The name "Vans" right away brings to mind *Fast Times at Ridgemont High* (1982), which features the legendary Vans Checkerboard Slip-On and its inimitable checkered motif.

Fast Times at Ridgemont High (1982)

Game of Death (1978)

Asics

Lastly, Asics, with its Onitsuka Tiger model, steals the scene in *Game of Death* (1978), starring Bruce Lee. In his yellow and black jumpsuit, the actor and martial artist dons a pair of Onitsuka Tiger Mexicos. Quentin Tarantino, who knows his classics, gave a very beautiful nod to Lee twenty-five years later in *Kill Bill: Volume 1* (2003), with Uma Thurman playing the role of Beatrix Kiddo. She too wore a yellow and black jumpsuit—and a pair of Onitsuka Tiger Tai Chi × Bruce Lee sneakers.

Kill Bill : Volume 1 (2003)

SCENE-STEALING PAIRS

FILMS HAVE IMMORTALIZED CERTAIN SNEAKERS! A COMPENDIUM

Nike Classic Cortez & *Forrest Gump* (1994)

Robert Zemeckis's film *Forrest Gump* is truly a masterpiece. One of the most memorable scenes is the one where Jenny (Robin Wright) gives a new pair of Nike Cortez sneakers to her friend Forrest Gump (Tom Hanks), who is obsessed with running. This scene has become so legendary that the Nike Classic Cortez in white, Varsity Red, and Varsity Royal Blue is now known as the "Forrest Gump."

Air Jordan IV OG "White Cement" (1989) & *Do the Right Thing* (1989)

If there is one person who really contributed to the success of Jordans, it is genius director Spike Lee. Whether in his films or the ads he made for Jordans, Spike Lee knew how to take advantage of the "coolitude" of pairs from this era. The director (and actor) even had his own model of Jordan IVs in 2006, with his character Mars Blackmon embroidered on the heel, in addition to the Air Spikes and Player Exclusives (PEs), not to mention the Spiz'ike.

In *Do the Right Thing*, one very funny scene shows Buggin Out (Giancarlo Esposito) and Clifton (John Savage) arguing because Clifton rolled over Buggin's new Jordan IV White Cements.

Spike Lee puts in a pair of Jordans that fits the times in all of his films—such as the previously mentioned Jordan XIIIs in *He Got Game* and, more recently, in the excellent *Da 5 Bloods*.

Spike and Michael Jordan are friends in real life, and it was that friendship that resulted in the Jordan Spiz'ikes in 2006. This Spike and Mike mash-up is one of the rare hybrid pairs that has been tolerated—and even loved by some collectors. A hybrid pair is a pair of sneakers that blends several models into one, in this case several Jordan Retros—Jordans III, IV, V, VI, IX, and XX. On the back of the Spiz'ike, you'll once again find the figure of Mars Blackmon, along with the famous logo of Spike Lee's production company, 40 Acres & A Mule Filmworks, whose name comes from an order issued during the American Civil War. The text provided for giving 40 acres and a mule to the freed slaves, but the promise was quickly revoked after Abraham Lincoln died.

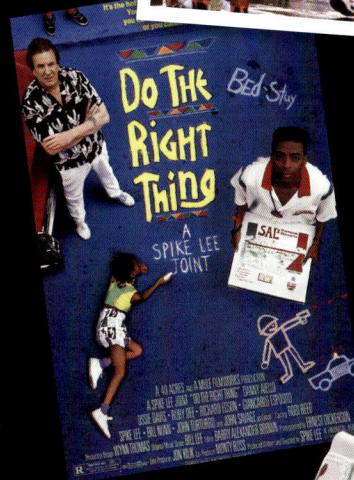

Jordan Spiz'ike

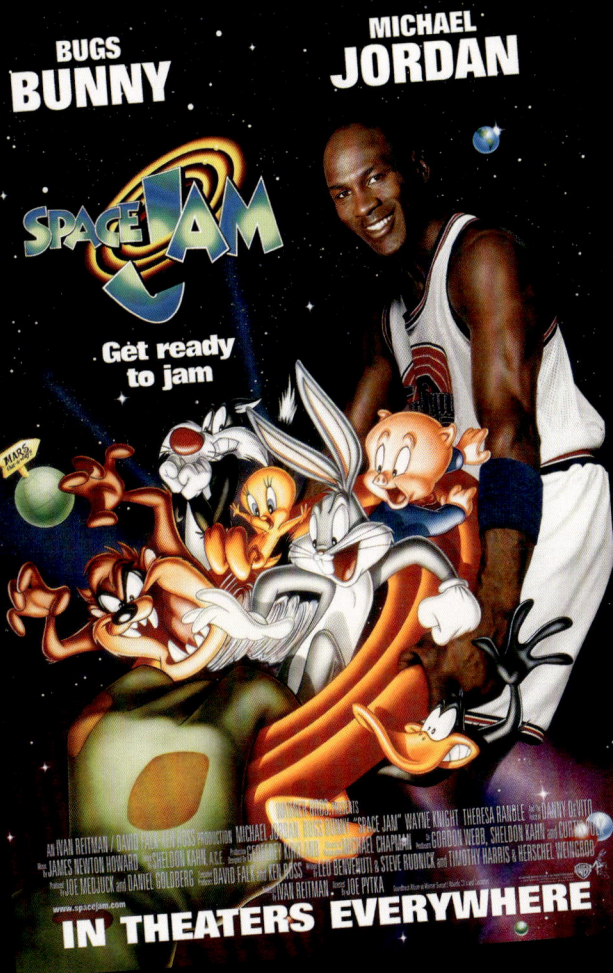

Air Jordan XI Retro "Space Jam" (2000) & *Space Jam* (1996)

This is the famous pair from the cult film *Space Jam* by Joe Pytka and Warner Bros. Family Entertainment! A novel, bold color scheme was created for this film, released in 1996. The shoe was sold for the first time in December 2000 and was enormously successful, especially in the American market. The rereleases that followed in 2009 and 2016 were likewise both hits. When the initial Jordan XI model came out in 1995, it was a minor success, but hardly more than that. It wasn't until the Jordan XI "Space Jam" launched in 2000 that the Jordan XIs became iconic in the United States.

For the 2016 release, a handful of lucky people received special "Space Jam" XI/XXXI packaging, just after the launch of the Air Jordan XXXI.

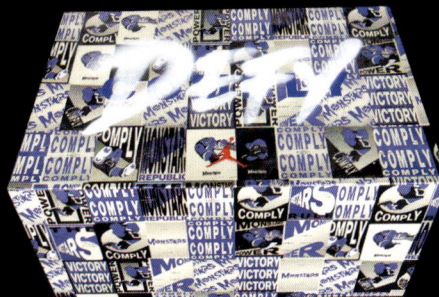

THE WINNER

Nike Mag & *Back to the Future II* (1989)

Nike Mag is the ultimate holy grail in the eyes of the large majority of sneaker addicts. This pair was designed by Tinker Hatfield for the Robert Zemeckis film *Back to the Future II* (1989), a remarkable science fiction comedy that is truly representative of the late eighties. In the film, Professor Emmett "Doc" Brown (Christopher Lloyd) gives Marty McFly (Michael J. Fox) a pair of Nike Mags so he can blend into the futuristic setting following the drive in the legendary DeLorean. Marty thus slips on a self-lacing pair and says, "Power laces! Alright!" The scene, and above all the sneakers, became an instant cult favorite!

On a sidenote, the Nike Mags in the film did not actually have automatic lacing: Two little invisible threads pulled from each side along with a nice little sound effect did that job. It was the first pair of sneakers in history that was entirely created for a movie.

Yet, the film was only the start of a long story, because everyone wanted those Nike Mags, both fans of the movie and sneakerheads. Nike and, more precisely, its executive chairman Mark Parker and designer Tinker Hatfield were well aware of the demand. However, the pair could not be sold because the automatic lacing technology was not up and running yet.

Never mind that! In 2011, the news broke: The Nike Mag would be sold! The news caused quite a stir, but the joy was short-lived because only 1,500 pairs ended up being produced and sold in the United States—and without those famous "power laces."

Nike Mag "Back to the Future II"
Release dates: 09/08/2011 and 10/04/2016
Resale of the 2011 model: $16,200–$32,400 (€15,000–€30,000) as of 2023
Resale of the 2016 model: $43,200–$86,400 (€40,000–€80,000) as of 2023

The sale was for a good cause, since all proceeds went to funding research on Parkinson's disease, from which, unfortunately, Michael J. Fox suffers. At that time, an incredible commercial aired in which you see, among others, the basketball player Kevin Durant, who wants to buy a pair of Nike Mags at a store in 2011. Suddenly, Professor Emmett Brown explodes into the store, asking the salesperson if the pair is indeed equipped with "power laces." The salesperson turns to the manager at the register (none other than Tinker Hatfield), who responds, "No, not before 2015." Lastly, the professor, who had messed up the year, sets off for 2015—more precisely, October 21, 2015, the date when Marty arrives in the future in the movie.

Come 2015, everyone was expecting a true reedition, but unfortunately, since the "power laces" system was still not ready, it didn't happen! Finally, in October 2016, the pair was sold with the "power laces." Alas, it was an extremely limited edition! Just eighty-nine pairs were produced and sold via a $10 lottery system in North America, at auction, and through a mini lottery at Nike Town London, with a single pair eligible to be won in Europe, still to benefit the Michael J. Fox Foundation. The good news is that, thanks to the 2011 and 2016 releases of this pair, the organizers had collected several millions of dollars for Parkinson's disease research.

This excellent initiative nevertheless caused prices on this model to explode at resale. Prices varied enormously depending on whether it was the 2011 or 2016 model, and sneakers that had been won via lottery or that were purchased at auction went for sums as high as $200,000, and even more.

The "power laces" system has really and truly existed since 2016 and is being sold at Nike. Other pairs integrating the Nike MAG DNA have been designed, and Tinker Hatfield still manages the "power laces" projects, although he's no longer the one designing every model. The current pairs are even more evolved than the ones in the film. You can customize tightness on the left and right, lights and batteries are controlled through an app on your phone or a connected watch, and there's still plenty of room for future innovations!

A TRIBUTE TO THE CINEMA

SNEAKERS INSPIRED BY FILMS

While the movies have celebrated and sanctified certain sneaker models, here are some shoes that have conversely paid enthusiastic tribute to film.

REEBOK

Reebok routinely creates pairs of sneakers in homage to films, usually in packs of several pairs, as with the *Jurassic Park* or *Kung Fu Panda* models. Quite often, Reebok incorporates its most iconic sneakers into these bold packs: for example, the Reebok Instapump Fury from Steven Smith, which came out in 1994. Two models have been particularly noteworthy in recent years: the "Ted" and the "Toy Story."

BAIT × Pixar × Reebok Instapump Fury "Buzz & Woody"

BAIT, a California retailer of collectible sneakers and clothing, very regularly releases collaborations with a large number of brands and businesses of all kinds, while always ensuring it preserves its own unique identity. The results are often sublime, such as this partnership with Pixar studios to create a pair for the animated film *Toy Story*, which came out in 1995. This pair is at the very least original, and it contains two different left and right shoes. The right shoe was done in the colors of Woody, and the left in the colors of Buzz Lightyear. The packaging was also very well executed—the pairs look like toys in their clear bags. The limited-edition sale took place exclusively at BAIT, by raffle. Winners got the chance to buy the pair of their dreams.

BAIT × Pixar × Reebok Instapump Fury "Buzz & Woody"

Release date: 06/13/2020
Retail price: $200
Resale: approximately $380 (€350) as of March 2023

BAIT × Pixar × Reebok Instapump Fury "Army Men"

Still in the spirit of *Toy Story*, a few lucky people received an even more limited edition of the "Army Men" pair, which was inspired by the plastic soldiers who commanded the army of soldiers in the animated film. Strangely, you can sometimes find pairs that cost less than $100. It's a steal for fans of the film and collectors alike!

BAIT × Pixar × Reebok Instapump Fury "Army Men"

Release date: 06/13/2020
Retail price: offered to select raffle winners for $200
Resale price: below retail price as of March 2023

BAIT × Reebok Instapump Fury "Happy Ted"

Released on the occasion of the film *Ted 2*, starring iconic actor Mark Wahlberg, this pair of sneakers, which was directly inspired by the hotheaded teddy bear Ted, is as bold as it is original. The shoe was once again sold exclusively at BAIT via raffle. An extremely limited edition of one hundred pairs coined "Nasty Ted," done in the image of the agitated bear himself, further drove demand. This version has a lower retail price than when it was released, which is surely because this type of model is probably less well known.

BAIT × Reebok Instapump Fury "Nasty Ted"

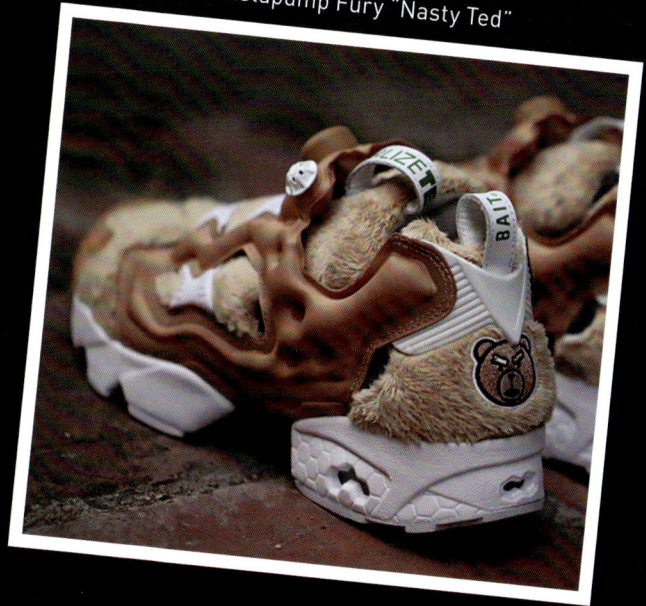

BAIT × Reebok Instapump Fury "Happy Ted"
Release date: 11/14/2015
Retail price: $170
Resale price: approximately $240 (€220) as of March 2023

ADIDAS

Adidas is also in the habit of designing pairs in tribute to films. Here are three incredible pairs that celebrate Christmas.

Adidas Forum Low "Home Alone"

As you'll see, the goal here is not only to present "hype" pairs but, above all, to showcase the sneakers that stand out from the crowd. This model is an homage to the quintessential Christmas movie—*Home Alone*, the 1990 Chris Columbus film starring a young Macaulay Culkin. These Adidas Forum Lows, released in 2021, are packed with film-related details. They come in a special box with three pairs of insoles, two of which are in the effigy of the "wet bandits," the film's pair of clumsy robbers (played by Joe Pesci and Daniel Stern). The pair also has traces of burning, as if firecrackers had exploded in spots, and even a shiny red M on the heel, recalling the scene where the young Kevin heats up the doorknob so the robbers burn their hands. My favorite detail? The patch on the tongue that looks like a welcome mat, with the Adidas logo on one foot and the logo of the film on the other. Lastly, note that this model reproduces the colors of the pair of Adidas Phantoms that protagonist Kevin wears in the 1990 film.

Adidas Forum Low "Home Alone"
Release date: December 2021
Sale price: $110
Resale price: below retail price as of March 2023

Adidas Forum Low "Home Alone II"

One year later, in 2022, Adidas honored the second opus, *Home Alone II* (which came out in 1992), with a touching tribute. This pair was inspired by the part when Kevin meets the "pigeon lady" at the foot of the Gapstow Bridge in Central Park, an iconic scene that signals the start of a touching friendship. The pair is in tonal gray, with a washed burgundy liner—the colors of a pigeon. The shoes feature a series of custom graphic hang tags, mismatched tongue tags with the words "Home Alone 2" and "Adidas," interchangeable lace jewels, and three pairs of shoelaces. Beneath the Velcro are the words "As long as we each have our turtledove, we'll be friends forever," in reference to one of the most moving lines of the film.

Adidas Forum Low "Home Alone II"

Release date: 12/03/2022
Sale price: $120
Resale price: below retail price as of March 2023

Adidas Stan Smith Gore-Tex "Gremlins Mogwai"

This pair is truly a gem: Discreetly released in 2020 for the Christmas holidays, it has remained on the Adidas website for a long time, probably because they're not easy to wear. The model references *Gremlins*, a classic 1984 Christmas movie directed by Joe Dante with a script by Chris Columbus (the director of *Home Alone*). The pair is directly inspired by the little Mogwai, Gizmo. The most striking detail (and the most original) is the reproduction of Gizmo's eyes on the heels. The shoes are in beige and maroon "pony hair" to recall the Mogwai's fur, and they contain the necessary rules for taking care of Mogwais on the insoles: Keep them out of sunlight, don't get them wet, and, most importantly, don't feed them after midnight!

The concern for detail was even extended to the design of the box, which re-created the patterns of the wrapping paper that Rand wrapped Gizmo in as a gift for his son, Billy, on Christmas Day.

Adidas Stan Smith Gore-Tex "Gremlins Mogwai"
Release date: 12/19/2020
Sale price: $120
Resale price: approximately $216 (€200) as of March 2023

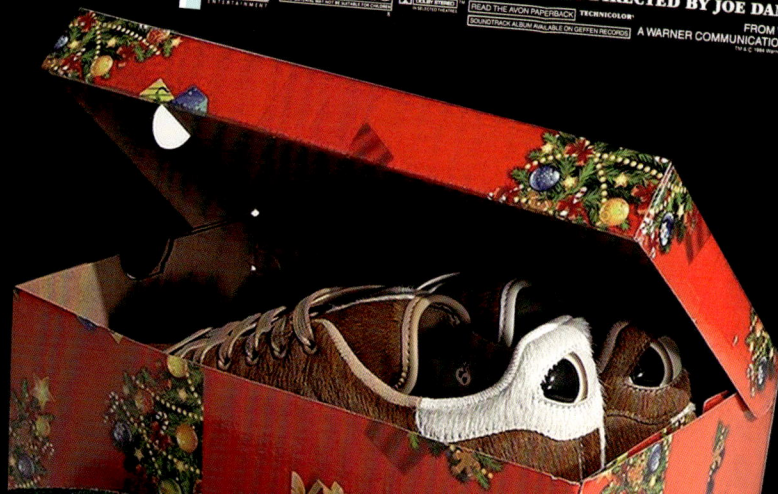

Cute.
Clever.
Mischievous.
Intelligent.
Dangerous.

STEVEN SPIELBERG
PRESENTS

GREMLINS

STARRING ZACH GALLIGAN
PHOEBE CATES·HOYT AXTON·POLLY HOLLIDAY·FRANCES LEE McCAIN
MUSIC BY JERRY GOLDSMITH·EXECUTIVE PRODUCERS STEVEN SPIELBERG·
FRANK MARSHALL·KATHLEEN KENNEDY·WRITTEN BY CHRIS COLUMBUS·
PRODUCED BY MICHAEL FINNELL·DIRECTED BY JOE DANTE
FROM WARNER BROS
A WARNER COMMUNICATIONS COMPANY

Reebok Alien Stomper Final Battle Double Pack

Even though they are not original pairs from the film *Aliens* (James Cameron, 1986), this "tribute pack" is really a treasure both for sneaker collectors and *Alien* fans. Only fifty packs were produced for this extremely limited edition. Pairs of each shoe were also sold individually, although single pairs are not worth nearly as much.

Chris Hill and Xavier Jones designed this pack.

Reebok Alien Stomper Final Battle Double Pack / "Power Loader" (yellow) / "Queen" (black patent leather)
Release date: 07/18/2017 Sale price: $325 Resale: approximately $594 (€550) as of March 2023

These two pairs were directly inspired by the queen alien and the legendary exoskeleton from the movie—the Power Loader P-5000:

• The "Queen Alien" model is made of black patent leather, which mimics the viscous look of the aliens' skin, with "green glow" accents that recall the queen alien's blood. To top it off, the code "XX121" that was given to the extraterrestrials is embroidered on the front of the shoe.

• The "Power Loader" model is an orangey-yellow color with black stripes and red arrows, reminiscent of the vehicle Ripley drives in the final fight.

As for the packaging, it too points to the scene when Ripley activates the doors in the loading area and ejects the queen alien from the vessel. This pack was really designed down to the tiniest detail!

• The "Reebok Stomper" High corresponds to the original model in the film. It was made in 1986 for the director of the first *Alien* (1979), Ridley Scott, who then passed the baton to his colleague James Cameron. The public discovered these Reebok Stompers onscreen, on the feet of actress Sigourney Weaver, a.k.a. Ellen Ripley. The pair was rereleased in 2016 in a pack made for Alien Day, which celebrated the thirtieth anniversary of *Aliens*, the sequel to *Alien*. Five hundred packs were sold at $175 each (one hundred came in a special box). As far as resale is concerned, prices vary enormously and can reach as much as several thousands of dollars—and even more for the special box version.

For the Mid version in the original colorway, 1,986 pairs were sold (in reference to the year 1986, when the second movie was released) for $135 each. As with the High version, resale prices can vary quite a bit and sometimes reach as much as several hundreds—or even thousands—of dollars.

THEMED
SNEAKERS

A PASSION
FOR SNEAKERS

There are incredibly romantic pairs in celebration of Valentine's Day!

NEW BALANCE

Joe Freshgoods × New Balance 992 / OMN1S "No Emotions Are Emotions" Pack

As far as New Balance goes, I must mention the amazing collection "No Emotions Are Emotions," a collaboration with Joe Freshgoods, a Chicago designer who put a new spin both on the 992s and the New Balance OMN1S, the professional model worn by Kawhi Leonard.

The complete set was released for the NBA All-Star Weekend in Chicago, held from Valentine's Day, February 14, to February 16, 2020. Joe Freshgoods thus killed two birds with one stone with this duo (truly a declaration of love to New Balance), while paying lively tribute to the world of basketball with the OMN1S.

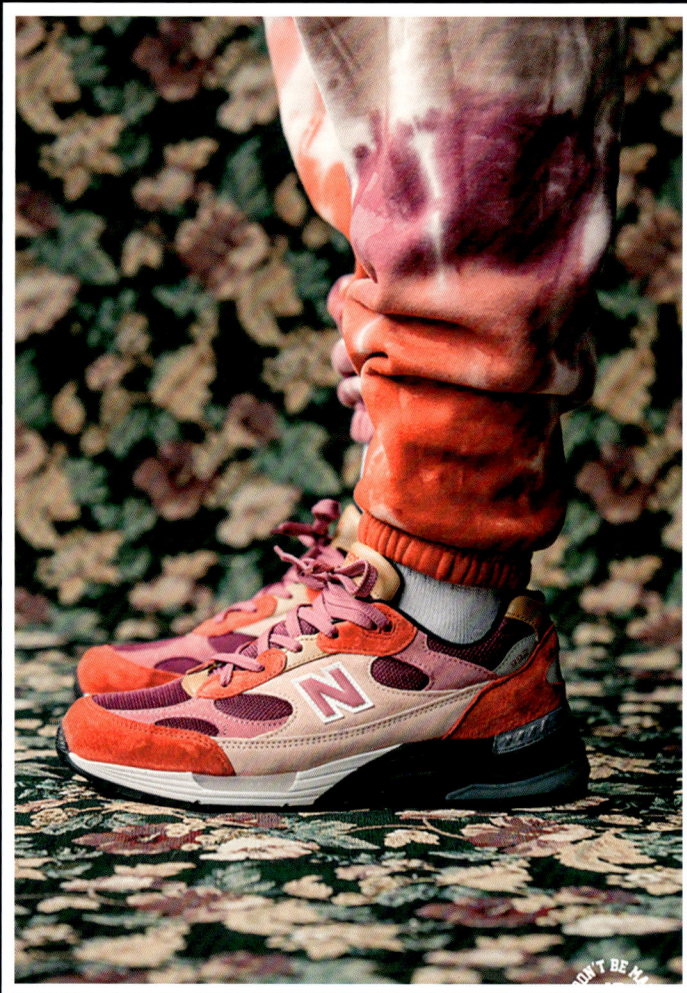

Joe Freshgoods × New Balance 992 / OMN1S "No Emotions Are Emotions" Pack

Release date: 02/14/2020
Sale price Joe Freshgoods × New Balance 992: $175
Sale price Joe Freshgoods × New Balance OMN1S: $180
Resale price Joe Freshgoods × New Balance 992:
   approximately $2,160 (€2,000) as of March 2023
Resale price Joe Freshgoods × New Balance OMN1S:
   approximately $325 (€300) as of March 2023

REEBOK

Reebok Question Mid Valentine's Day 2015

Reebok really ran with the Valentine's Day theme (and to superb effect) with the Reebok Question Mid Valentine's Day, released in February 2015. Recall that the Question Mid is the professional model worn by Allen Iverson, a true NBA legend. The pair has its place in the pantheon of sneakers—just as Allen Iverson has his place in the Hall of Fame.

Reebok Question Mid Valentine's Day 2015

Release date: 02/09/2015
Sale price: $95
Resale price: Unknown

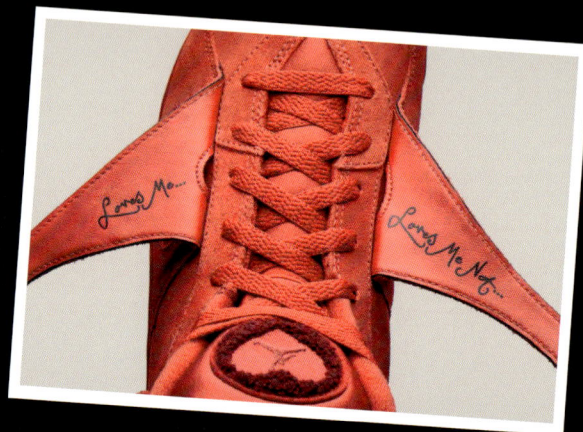

NIKE

At Nike there is truly an embarrassment of riches for Valentine's Day! Indeed, the American giant (and market leader) has capitalized on this theme for several dozen years running. However, if we're focusing on the nicest pairs, then two models stand out: the Air Jordan VIII Retro Valentine's Day from 2018, definitely a feast for the eyes, and the Strangelove × Nike SB Dunk Low Valentine's Day from 2020, which is the Valentine's Day pair most in demand at resale and thus the undisputed winner!

Air Jordan VIII Retro Valentine's Day (W) 2018

Release date: 02/09/2018
Sale price: $190
Resale: approximately $380 (€350) as of March 2023

THE WINNER

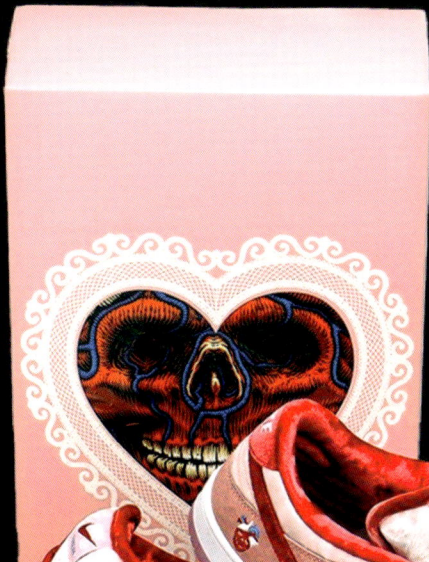

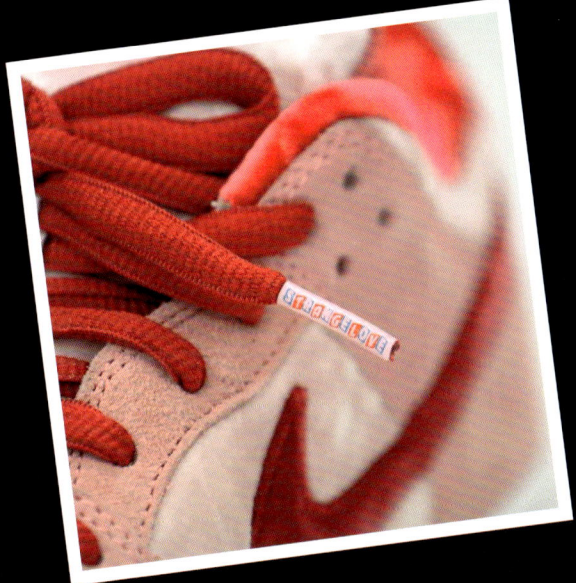

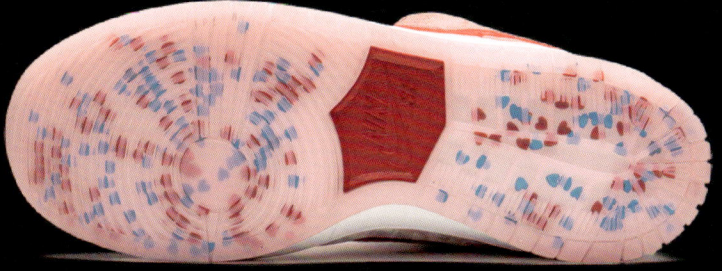

Strangelove × Nike SB Dunk Low Valentine's Day (Special Box)

- Release date: 02/01/2020
- Sale price: $100
- Resale price of regular box: approximately $1,300 (€1,200) as of March 2023
- Resale of special box: approximately $2,160 (€2,000) as of March 2023

SNEAKERS—THE "EASTER SPECIAL"

THE NICEST PAIRS FOR EASTER SUNDAY!

No, you're not dreaming! There are fabulous Easter-themed pairs.

REEBOK

Reebok Classic Kamikaze II and Question Mid "His and Hers" Easter Pack

As far as Reebok is concerned, it's interesting to point out the "His and Hers" Easter Pack Reebok Classic, an original set from 2014 consisting of a pair of "Question Mids" and a pair of "Kamikaze IIs," both of which originally came out in 1996.

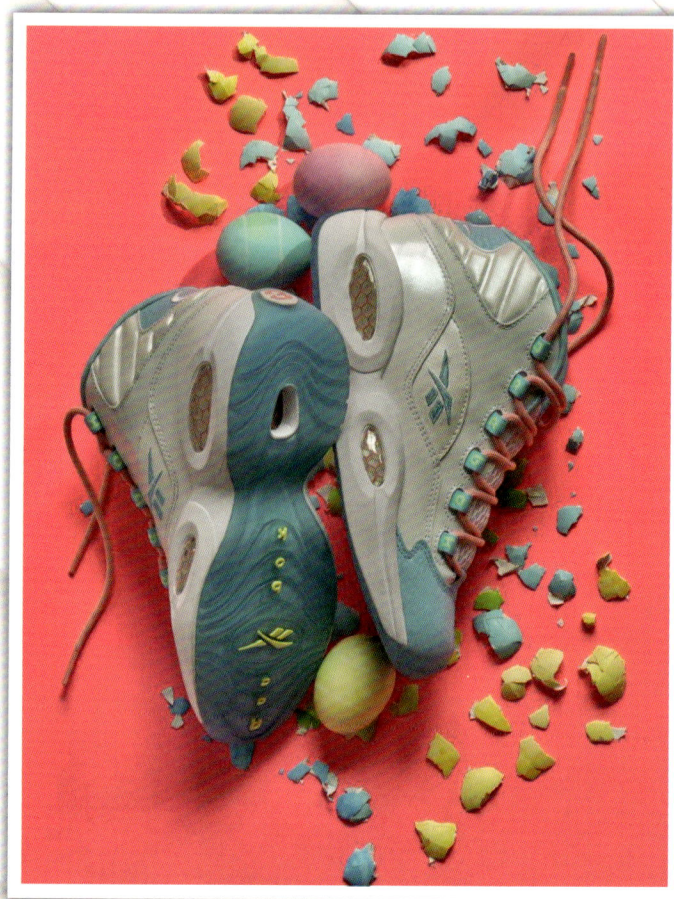

Reebok Classic Kamikaze II and Question Mid "His and Hers" Easter Pack

Release date: 04/18/2014
Kamikaze II retail price: $100
Question Mid retail price: $95
Resale price: Unknown

NEW BALANCE

New Balance M1500MPK/M1500MGK "Easter Pastel" Pack Made in England

As for New Balance, it's the "Easter Pastel" Pack, released as a limited edition in 2017, that stands out. The set is composed of one pair of NB M1500MPKs and a pair of M1500MGKs, made in England and fresh out of the Flimby factories (which is truly a mark of quality).

New Balance M1500MPK/M1500MGK "Easter Pastel" Pack Made in England
Release date: 04/26/2017
Retail price: €160
Resale price: Unknown

NIKE

It's harder to choose the frontrunner from Nike because their Easter offerings have been so vast. Almost every model has an "Easter" version, in particular the b-ball pairs such as the Kevin Durants, Kyries, Lebrons, etc. To narrow the playing field, let's focus on the pairs that stand out from the crowd, be it for their popularity or how they are made.

Nike Air Force 1 Low "Easter Egg"

When we talk about Easter-themed sneakers, this pair is the shoe of reference. First released in 2005, the sneakers benefited from a rerelease in 2017 (shown opposite). Additionally, the AF1 Low Easter Egg of 2006 always has a high value. It was released in an Easter pack with the Nike Air Max 180 Easter Egg, which is now somewhat rare.

Nike Air Force 1 Low "Easter Egg"
Release date: April 2005
Rerelease date: 04/17/2017
Retail price: $170
Resale price: $490 (€450) as of March 2023

Nike Dunk High Easter Polka Dot (QS)

You have to admire this Quickstrike* (in other words, a very limited edition, especially in 2007, because quantities were even more limited than today). This model embodies chocolate Easter bunnies, which you can moreover see on the insoles and tongue.

Nike Dunk High Easter Polka Dot (QS)
Release date: 03/31/2017
Sale price: $125
Resale price: $430 (€400) as of March 2023 (provided you can find your size)

*Quickstrike (QS): An edition that is limited in terms of both space and time; these editions are sold exclusively at certain boutiques and for a limited period.

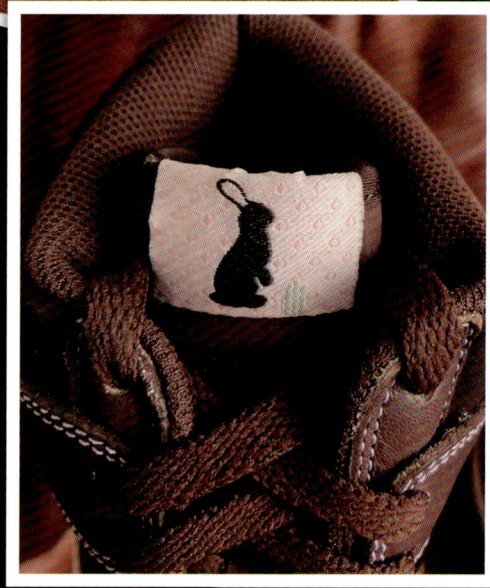

Nike Kobe 10 "Easter"

After Kobe Bryant's tragic death in a helicopter crash on January 26, 2020, the value of Nike Kobe models shot through the roof. The craze has now settled down somewhat, although certain models have inevitably become more popular. There are several Easter-themed Kobe pairs, although we'll focus here on this turquoise-colored, robin's-egg-inspired model.

Nike Kobe 10 "Easter"
Release date: 04/02/2015
Sale price: $180
Resale price: $540 (€500) as of March 2023

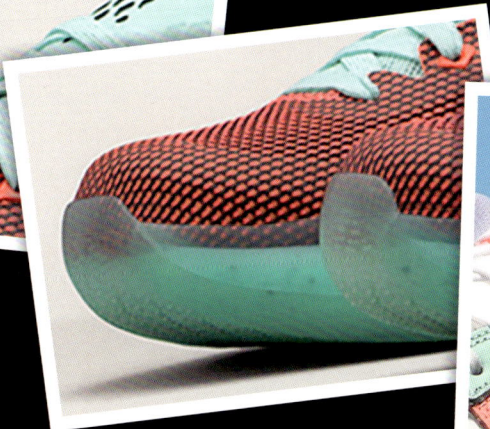

Nike Dunk Low WMNS "Easter Candy"

This pair picks up the pastel colorway of traditional Easter egg wrappers, in the same spirit as the 2005 Air Force 1s. In 2021, Dunks were super trendy for women, and this model was especially made for the ladies—the shoe's popularity explains why it made this list.

Nike Dunk Low WMNS "Easter Candy"
Release date: 05/25/2021
Sale price: $110
Resale price: $325 (€300) as of March 2023

ADIDAS

Bad Bunny × Adidas Forum Low "Easter Egg"

One Adidas model by far surpasses the brand's other Easter-inspired pairs. It's a collaboration with Puerto Rican artist Bad Bunny, who reinvented a Forum Low as a skater-style shoe. Generally speaking, collaborations between Bad Bunny and Adidas have been extremely successful!

Bad Bunny × Adidas Forum Low "Easter Egg"
Release date: 04/04/2021 (an Easter Sunday)
Sale price: $140
Resale price: $700 (€650) as of March 2023

SCARY
SNEAKERS!

HALLOWEEN KICKS

As with the other categories of shoes featured in this book, there's an enormous number of pairs on the almost inexhaustible theme of Halloween. I've therefore chosen to show you the ones I like most, along with, of course, some other quintessential pairs that celebrate this spooky holiday.

A Bathing Ape BAPE STA Low "Halloween Mummy"

Release date: 10/31/2006
Retail price: $200
Resale price: Unknown

A Bathing Ape BAPE STA Low "Halloween Orange"

Release date: 10/31/2006
Retail price: $200
Resale price: Unknown

A Bathing Ape BAPE STA Low "Halloween Black Orange"

Release date: 10/31/2006
Retail price: $200
Resale price: Unknown

BAPE Halloween Pack 2006

Released as a limited edition for Halloween 2006, these pairs are now quite difficult to find, particularly as deadstock or in good condition. These shoes all feature the patent leather BAPE is known for, along with bold colors. The white version was nicknamed "the Mummy" due to the BAPE logo on the heel: a monkey head wrapped in white strips of cloth. The orange version featured the traditional colors of the holiday, with the monkey head logo, this time carved like a pumpkin and customized for the occasion. The green model was done in the colors of the famous Frankenstein's monster, incorporating the logo into the theme; the same was true for the red, which was coined "Dracula." Such a great pack!

A Bathing Ape BAPE STA Low "Halloween Dracula"

Release date: 10/31/2006
Retail price: $200
Resale price: Unknown

A Bathing Ape BAPE STA Low "Halloween Frankenstein"

Release date: 10/31/2006
Retail price: $200
Resale price: Unknown

Le Coq Sportif "LCS" R800 "*Ça*" ("It") Fear Pack

This pair forms a two-pack with the R1000s. This shoe is inspired by the horrifying clown "It." The R800 model, which looks fairly simple, has a white and red colorway. The face of the clown murderer lurks under its translucent sole.

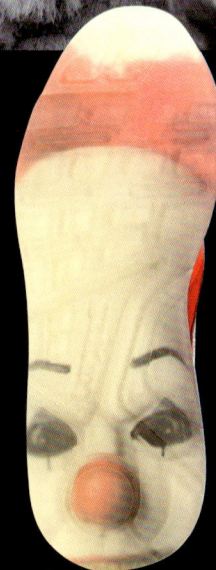

Le Coq Sportif "LCS" R800 "Ça" Fear Pack
Release date: October 2016
Retail price: €120
Resale price: Unknown

Alife × Asics Gel-Lyte III Monster Pack

Our New Yorker friends at Alife had fun working on this *Godzilla*-inspired 2007 collaboration. Released as a limited edition the same year, there is also an F&F shoe in a white version.

Alife × Asics Gel-Lyte III Monster Pack
Release date: October 2007
Retail price: $200
Resale price: $215–$1,080 (€200–€1,000) as of June 2023

Saucony Grid 9000 "Hallowed" Pack

A very simple Saucony pack coined "Hallowed," because the two pairs were released for the Halloween season. The tiny stains on the soles provide that touch of eccentricity. I really like this model!

Saucony Grid 9000 "Hallowed" Pack
Release date: October 2015
Retail price: $80 (each)
Resale price: Unknown

Adidas Forum Low "Scary Clown"

A bloody pair that pays tribute to the terrifying clown It. With this model, the three-stripe brand was a bit heavy-handed, but I think the result is pretty cool. The pair is packed with details, such as the delicately drawn tonal teeth in red leather at the front of the shoe.

Adidas Forum Low "Scary Clown"

Release date: 10/31/2020
Retail price: $110
Resale price: $140–$300 (€130–€280) as of June 2023

Adidas "Night of the Ballin' Dead" Pack

The theme is clear on these three excellent b-ball pairs from Adidas: zombies—with tonal brain patterns in flashy colors with splatters of a viscous mixture that glows in the dark. These pairs definitely stand out from the crowd!

Adidas "Night of the Ballin' Dead" Pack

Release date: 10/31/2015
Retail price:
D Rose 6: $140
D Lillard 1: $105
Crazy 8: $110
Resale price: Unknown

Adidas Original Superstar Halloween

There are several different Halloween-themed Adidas Superstars. This one is cool, has festive colors, and features a pumpkin on the tongue and an orange liner: simple and effective!

Adidas Original Superstar Halloween
Release date: October 2002 Retail price: $100 Resale price: Unknown

Reebok × Ghostbuster "Ghost Smasher" Pack

Still on the theme of *Ghostbusters*, a franchise that Reebok has regularly borrowed from, here's the "Ghost Smasher," the same model as for *Alien*. You may surmise that the pair has been designed to mimic the proton blaster of the film with the famous logo, which you'll find on the tongue. In 2022, a new version of the pair was released, with a few differences, for the DVD release of *Ghostbusters: Afterlife*.

Reebok × Ghostbuster "Ghost Smasher" Pack
Release date: 10/31/2020 Retail price: $150 Resale price: $216 (€200) as of June 2023

Bait × Stranger Things × Reebok Ex-O-Fit Clean Hi Ghostbusters

The now-famous Los Angeles store Bait has struck once again with this original collaboration, perfectly timed with the series *Stranger Things*. Bait is definitely always surprising us with its big-name collabs! Here, the choice of model fits the era of the series—in this case, the shoes feature *Ghostbusters* drawings by Dustin Henderson, who plays a fan of the franchise's films in the TV series. There is also a more limited vintage version.

Bait × Stranger Things × Reebok Ex-O-Fit Clean Hi Ghostbusters
Release date: 11/04/2017 Retail price: $140 Resale price: $216 (€200) as of June 2023

Reebok × Ghostbuster Classic Leather Pack

A Reebok Classic Leather model that's far from staid! This shoe is sold in a pack with the "Ghost Smasher" model opposite.

Reebok × Ghostbuster Classic Leather Pack
Release date: 10/31/2020 Retail price: $100 Resale price: $130–$280 (€120–€260) as of June 2023

Reebok "Boktober" Pack

They love to have fun over at Reebok, especially with retro pairs. To start, there's the Shaqnosis, which is covered with a spiderweb on a glow-in-the-dark outsole. Next is the Kamikaze II, which received the Jack-O-Kaze orange and black treatment. Lastly, there's the Question Mid "Ankle Reaper," which contains a cutaway upper that reveals a creepy Halloween print underneath. It also has tombstones on the heels inscribed with the word "Ankle" and some glow-in-the-dark components. A super-nice pack!

Reebok "Boktober" Pack
Release date: 10/14/2020 Retail price: Shaqnosis "Webs": $140 Question Mid "Ankle Reaper": $150 Kamikaze II "Jack-O-Kaze": $120 Resale price: Shaqnosis "Webs": $215 (€200) Question Mid "Ankle Reaper" and Kamikaze II "Jack-O-Kaze": under retail price as of June 2023

Reebok Pump Omni Lite Pumpkin Halloween Pack

A really nice, limited-edition sneaker that was released for Halloween 2013! This pumpkin-colored Pump features glow-in-the-dark beehive components that light up the pair like jack-o'-lanterns with candles inside. The shoe forms part of a pack with the Kamikaze II "Acid Rain." The whole top portion of the shoe is entirely glow-in-the-dark, which mimics the look of acid rain.

Reebok Pump Omni Lite Pumpkin Halloween Pack
Release date: 10/25/2013 Retail price: $120 Resale price: Unknown

Reebok The Blast "Halloween"

This Reebok rerelease of the "Blast," a retro pair from the 1990s made popular by people such as Nick Van Exel, otherwise known as "Nick the Quick," is Halloween personified. It's a spectacular pair with an explosive design, covered by a red splatter that looks like a splash of blood.

Reebok The Blast "Halloween"
Release date: 10/31/2014 Retail price: $120 Resale price: Unknown

Reebok Instapump Fury OG "Halloween"

The Reebok Instapump Fury OG Halloween from 2016 is a somber, studded, almost gothic pair of sneakers. There's no particular storyline behind this shoe, but its atypical and unique design makes it worth mentioning.

Reebok Instapump Fury OG "Halloween"
Release date: October 2016 Retail price: $175 Resale price: Unknown

Vans Horror Pack 2021 × Warner Bros

I loved this Horror pack when it came out, and I still love it today! It contains nine pairs (not all of which are pictured) in tribute to classic Warner Bros. horror films such as *A Nightmare on Elm Street*, *It*, *The Exorcist*, *Friday the 13th*, *The Shining*, and *The Lost Boys*. Each model has a special box in the likeness of the corresponding film. My three favorite pairs are the Jason Voorhees Vans Slip-Ons, in tribute to *Friday the 13th*, followed by "The Shining" Vans Slip-Ons featuring the twins on the front and the final bouquet, and the "Nightmare on Elm Street" shoe, patterned (as is the box) to look like the antihero's bloodstained sweaters. Special nod to Vans for this amazing pack, which I'm sure delighted both sneakerheads and fans of classic horror movies.

Vans Horror Pack 2021 × Warner Bros

Release date: October 2021
Retail price: $80 on average
Resale price: around $216 (€200) as of June 2023 for the "Nightmare on Elm Street" model. Most other pairs go for under retail price.

Size? × Vans Sk8-Hi 38 DX Halloween

Generally speaking, the British retailer Size often offers us nice, novel, and exclusive collaborations. This pair is no exception. Punchy details include the bones on the sole, yellow accents, pupils on the Vans logo that trickle down from the liner, spiderwebs, and laces sporting the words "trick" and "treat." A truly awesome pair of Vans!

Size? × Vans Sk8-Hi 38 DX Halloween

Release date: 10/25/2019
Retail price: £75
Resale price: $216 (€200)

Nike Air Force 1 Low Skeleton

Although recent, this super-successful model will definitely become a classic. The idea is simple, and the result is cool. A foot skeleton makes it look as though the shoes were going through an x-ray machine, a motif that's also found on the insole. Nike took the concept all the way to the patch on the tongue, which has the Nike logo embroidered in bones. Bonus point for the outsole, which glows in the dark. As you can see, a Skeleton pack has taken shape over the years.

Nike Air Force 1 Low Skeleton "White"

Release date: 10/31/2018
Retail price: $100
Resale price: $325–$750 (€300–€700) as of June 2023

Nike Air Force 1 Low Skeleton "Black"

Release date: 10/25/2019
Retail price: $130
Resale price: $325–$540 (€300–€500) as of June 2023

Nike Air Force 1 Low Skeleton "Orange"

Release date: 10/28/2020
Retail price: $130
Resale price: approximately $162 (€150) as of June 2023

Nike Air Force 1 Low Skeleton "Purple"

Release date: 04/01/2022
Retail price: $130
Resale price: $140–$216 (€130–€200) as of June 2023

Nike Air Force 1 Low PRM Halloween 2005

There are many Halloween-themed AF1s, with exclusive models and very popular limited editions like the one pictured here, which are currently extremely difficult to find in good condition. This model is part of a pack of two with another pair of patent leather AF1s, but with one orange side and one black side. A monstrous face appears on the tongue and heel, held by a skeleton hand. A skeleton hand and arm also appear on the sole.

Nike Air Force 1 Low PRM Halloween 2005

Release date: October 2005
Retail price: $100
Resale price: approximately $430 (€400) as of June 2023

Air Force 1 Low Shibuya Halloween

This unique Japanese exclusive features transparent components, a Halloween colorway, patent and grainy leathers, and a silhouetted skyline of the city of Shibuya, with the inscribed letters SBY(for Shibuya). It's a very beautiful AF1 to have in your collection. Shibuya is the nerve center of Japanese and international fashion, where Halloween is celebrated to the great joy of the Japanese.

Nike Air Force 1 Low Shibuya Halloween
Release date: 10/30/2019 Retail price: $140 Resale price: $140–$215 (€130–€200) as of June 2023

Nike Air Force 1 Low Frankenstein

An exceptional AF1! At a time when the sneaker craze was not at the point it is now, this pair seemed like a curiosity due to its theme: the famous Frankenstein's monster. The shoe forms part of Nike's "Frankenstein Family" pack and comes with a WMNS version for women and a pair of "Vandals" for the kids. This pair is in flashy patent leather in monster colors, with "scars" here and there.

Nike Air Force 1 Low Frankenstein
Release date: October 2006 Retail price: $190 Resale price: $325–$540 (€300–€500) as of June 2023

Nike Dunk Low Mummy

A true embalmed mummy! This pair speaks for itself, with its beige, lightly distressed canvas, stitching here and there, glow-in-the-dark mummy eyes on the heels, and hieroglyphs under the tongue.

Nike Dunk Low Mummy
Release date: 10/28/2021 Retail price: $110 Resale price: $325–$595 (€300–€550) as of June 2023

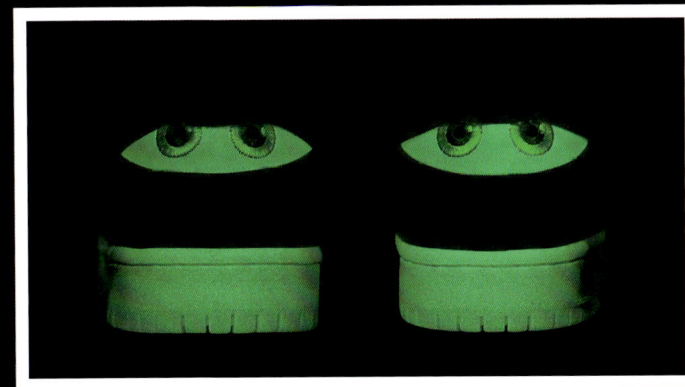

FREDDY KRUEGER

Nike Air Max 95 "Freddy Krueger"

This type of shoe really shows us how the sneaker game has evolved! In 2007, Nike was forced to cancel the sale of the legendary Nike SB Dunk Low "Freddy Krueger" (see the next page for that story) at the studio's request. Now that we are in a completely different time, movie franchises appreciate sneakers that pay homage to movies.

The Nike Air Max 95 "Freddy Krueger" is inspired by the clothes worn by Wes Craven's burned killer. As far as the details go, I particularly like the checked wool design on the tongue, the bubbles of blood in the exterior air bubble underneath the shoe, and, above all, the parts that look like bloody metal located on the heel and shoelace holes.

Nike Air Max 95 "Freddy Krueger"
Release date: 10/30/2020
Retail price: $170
Resale price: $216–$380 (€200–€350) as of June 2023

Nike SB Dunk High Pro "Jason Voorhees"

The colorway on this model is a tribute to the movie *Friday the 13th* and particularly to Jason Voorhees, the killer. I love the distressed and bloody, almost dirty, feel of the pair, which really fits the killer. On paper, this sneaker is nothing special, but over time it's become a classic SB.

Nike SB Dunk High Pro "Jason Voorhees"
Release date: 10/27/2007
Retail price: $90
Resale price: $1,600–$2,700 (€1,500–€2,500) as of June 2023

Nike SB Dunk Low Pro "Freddy Krueger"

Originally, this pair (a subtle wink at the film *A Nightmare on Elm Street*) was scheduled to be released in a so-called Horror pack for Halloween 2007. However, it turned out that Freddy Krueger's striped sweater was a registered trademark of New Line Cinema. After several unsuccessful attempts at negotiation, Nike was forced to cancel the sale, even though these sneakers had already been produced and, in some cases, already been delivered to the stores, ready to be sold. Nike thus sent the pairs back to the warehouses to be destroyed. Apparently, a Mexican skate shop had already sold its pairs early by mistake, and one employee had supposedly also succeeded in stealing several pairs before they were destroyed. We'll never know the truth, but one thing's for sure: There are extremely few real "Freddy Krueger" pairs in circulation. As far as technical components go, the shoes feature mesh mimicking the stripes on Freddy's sweater, a Swoosh that represents the sharp claws of the killer, and flesh-colored, "bloodstained" leather.

Nike SB Dunk Low Pro "Freddy Krueger"

Release date: 2007
Retail price: not sold
Resale price: $11,800–$32,400 (€11,000–€30,000) as of 2023

Nike Cortez "Día de los Muertos"

Inspired by the similarly themed 2015 Cortez sneakers, this model has a more somber look, which I personally prefer. The shoe incorporates the orange and black Halloween colors but with a slightly smoky look. White tonal details on the Swoosh and insole feature Mexican folklore motifs. The sneaker is also known as "Day of the Dead."

Nike Cortez "Día de los Muertos"

Release date: 10/15/2019
Retail price: $120
Resale price: $160–$430 (€150–€400) as of June 2023

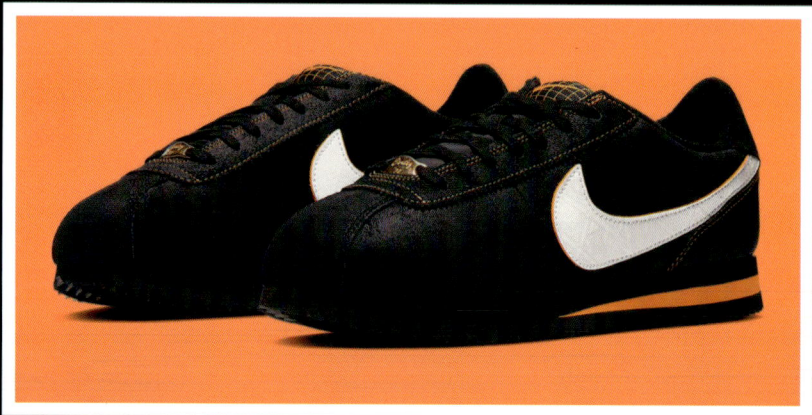

Off-White × Nike Blazer Mid "All Hallows Eve"

These sneakers provide a beautiful memory of Virgil Abloh, who was inspired by the colors of Halloween when designing this pair (released during that period). Although officially named the "Mid Vanilla," they were nicknamed "All Hallows' Eve" (the word "Halloween" is actually a contraction of "All Hallows Eve," which comes from the "Eve of All Hallows' Day"). This model builds on the standard features used in the collaborations between Nike and Virgil Abloh's brand Off-White.

Off-White × Nike Blazer Mid "All Hallows Eve"

Release date: 10/03/2018
Retail price: $130
Resale price: $540–$975 (€500–€900) as of June 2023

Nike Lebron 13 "Friday 13th" Halloween

Lebron's professional models cover all the holidays, or nearly all, and Halloween is often the theme of new pairs. Here's a great "bloodstained" Nike Lebron 13. It's also known as the "Friday the 13th" or even as the "Horror Flick." An amazing pair for collectors of Lebron models!

Nike Lebron 13 "Friday the 13th" Halloween

Release date: 11/13/2015
Retail price: $200
Resale price: $216–$540 (€200–€500) as of June 2023

FOOD
ADDICTS

THE PAIRS ON THE MENU!

Sneakers that champion every category of cooking? They actually exist! Food is a vast theme that has inspired many sneakers. Pairs vying to be the most original have succeeded in making us drool. Here's an overview of the most noteworthy models that have taken up this divine theme.

MODELS THAT ARE REALER THAN REAL!

Saucony often creates very successful sneakers that have been inspired by our food fetishes. Note the Dunkin' Donuts × Saucony Kinarava 10 (2018), the Saucony "Scoops of Ice Cream" Pack (2015), the Saucony Shadow 6000 "Avocado Toast" (2019), and the Saucony Shadow 6000 "New York Cheesecake" (2022).

Saucony Shadow 6000 "New York Cheesecake"

Saucony Shadow 6000 "Avocado Toast"

Converse has the Andy Warhol × Converse Chuck Taylor Collection (2015), which stands out from the crowd as a spin on the quintessential Campbell's soup so dear to the artist. As for Adidas, I really love the M&Ms × Adidas Originals Forum Low 84 pack (2022), for which six colorways in the shades of M&Ms were designed.

At Reebok, the 2019 "International Food" pack stands out, with three pairs, corresponding to three collaborations with some of the best German brands: Overkill, Asphaltgold, and 43einhalb. They include a Döner Kebab Reebok Classic Leather pair for Overkill, a Reebok Club C Revenge inspired by noodles by the chef Panda Rui Bù for 43einhalb, and a pizza-themed Reebok CL Nylon for Asphaltgold. All three models come in special packaging featuring their respective themes. A special nod goes to Le Coq Sportif, for its Le Coq Sportif R800 "Sorbet" packs (2018), composed of three colorful pairs inspired by three different flavors of ice cream.

M&Ms × Adidas Originals Forum Low 84

Krispy Kreme × Nike Kyrie 2 Ky-Rispy (Krispy) Kreme

Nike SB Dunk "Chicken and Waffles"

Nike SB Dunk Low "Street Hawker"

Social Status × Nike Dunk Mid Free Lunch Pack

Momofuku × Nike SB Dunk High Pro

Dinnertime!

To conclude, the quintessential Nike pairs in this subject area are the legendary Nike SB Dunk "Chicken and Waffles" (2016) in waffle-weave fabric; the Social Status × Nike Dunk Mid Free Lunch Pack (2019) in candy strawberry colors; the Momofuku × Nike SB Dunk High Pro (2017), a model directly inspired by the Momofuku Noodle Bar in New York in collaboration with the chef David Chang; the Nike SB Dunk Low "Street Hawker" (2021), which pays tribute to Chinese food; and the Krispy Kreme × Nike Kyrie 2 Ky-Rispy (Krispy) Kreme. This last pair benefited from a masterful communications campaign: A Krispy Kreme doughnut truck went to Cleveland, Baltimore, Harlem, and Brooklyn to distribute the pairs, packaged in clear doughnut boxes.

BURGERMANIA

END × Saucony Shadow 5000 "Burger"

Here's one of this brand's most popular collaborations. The famous London brand END Clothing took its inspiration from a hamburger when designing this pair, which is based on the Shadow 5000, an amazing model from 1985. Nubuck leather and perforated suede add lots of charm to this sneaker, done in the colors of the most famous sandwich in the world (green for the lettuce, beige for the bun, and red for the ketchup. With a gum sole stamped "END" and a hamburger on the tongue, the pair is sure to spark a reaction.

END × Saucony Shadow 5000 "Burger"
Release date: 05/01/2014
Retail price: €120
Resale price: $270–$750 (€250–€700) as of April 2023

A TASTE FOR BEIGNETS

Sneaker Politics × Café du Monde × Saucony Shadow 5000 "White"

Food is decidedly one of Saucony's favorite themes. This pair brings to mind the charm of Louisiana, and especially New Orleans. Sneaker Politics, the South's brand par excellence, teamed up with Saucony and a New Orleans institution, Café du Monde, which has been famous for its French beignets since the 1860s (anyone who goes to New Orleans *has* to visit Café du Monde). The pair was thus designed around this theme and in these colors, in yellow and burgundy, covered in white speckles to symbolize the powdered sugar that tops these famous beignets. There is a white version of this model, in a limited edition of 157 pairs, which is a nod to the 157 years that Café du Monde had been in operation. The maroon version, which is just as great, had a less limited release.

Both pairs come in a special box that looks like the café's beignet boxes, with cooking instructions on the back. These models are examples of extremely rare pairs that you can find at a very affordable price.

Sneaker Politics × Café du Monde × Saucony Shadow 5000 "White"
Release date: 06/22/2019
Retail price: $120
Resale price: $216–$650 (€200–€600) as of April 2023

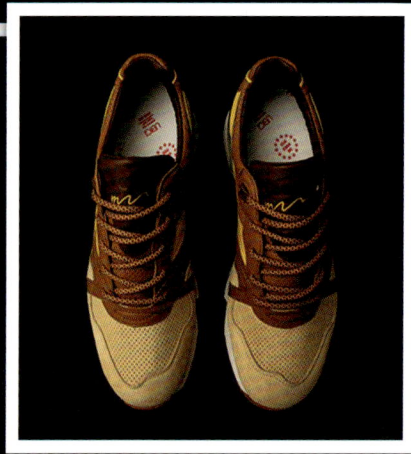

UBIQ × Diadora N9000 "Whiz Wit"

For this collaboration with Italian brands Diadora and UBIQ, the Philadelphia-based brand worked on a design in tribute to a local classic—the Philly cheesesteak—nicknamed the "Whiz Wit." This pair, stamped Whiz Wit and UBIQ, came out great and sports the colors of the delicious Philadelphia sandwich. First sold at UBIQ, it was also sold in small quantities in Europe and can sometimes be found under retail price.

UBIQ × Diadora N9000 "Whiz Wit"
Release date: 01/28/2017 Retail price: $190

WASABI INSPO

End × Asics Gel-Lyte III "Wasabi" (Special Box)

Here's a limited edition sold exclusively at End Clothing, which is one of the best boutiques in London. When designing these Asics Gel-Lyte IIIs, the British designers took their inspiration from wasabi (a plant that grows in Japan whose root is eaten in the form of a green paste as a condiment), all while ensuring a delicate, finely crafted finished product—just like Japanese cuisine. A true accomplishment!

End × Asics Gel-Lyte II "Wasabi" (Special Box)
Release date: 03/08/2018
Retail price: €140
Resale price: $270–$540 (€250-€500) as of April 2023

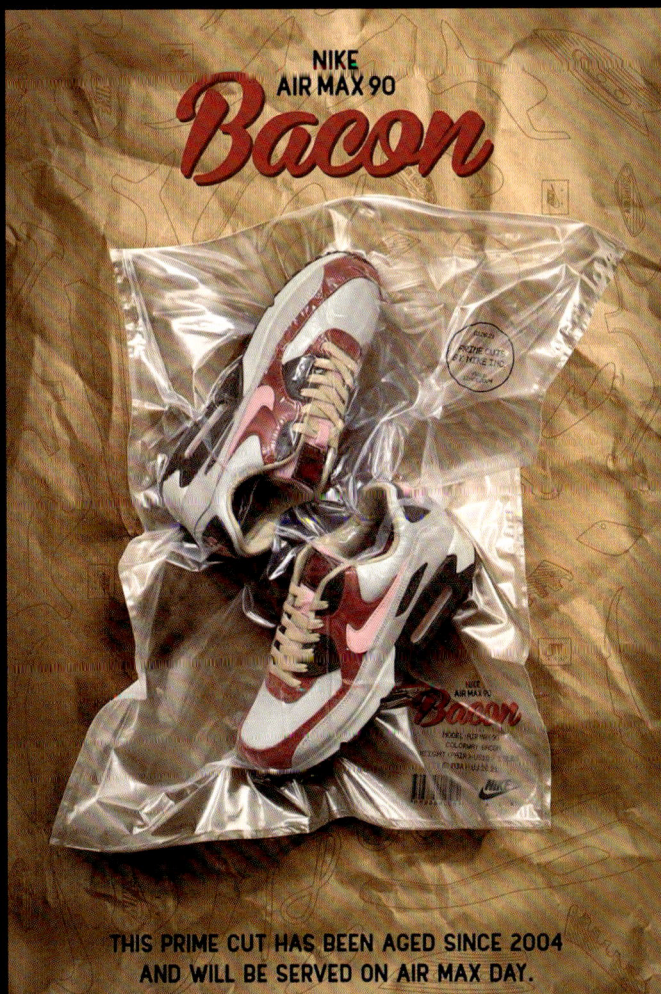

A PASSION FOR BACON

Daves Quality Meats × Nike Air Max 90 "Bacon"

The cornerstone of Air Max Day 2021 was the rerelease of an iconic and much-sought-after model from 2004. Daves Quality Meats × Nike Air Max 90 "Bacon" has a very interesting history. The shoe was a mockup, featuring a colorway designed by someone who didn't work for the brand—in this case David Ortiz, while he was owner of the concept store Dave's Quality Meats in Manhattan (now closed). It was a skate shop and sneaker store where the products were presented as if they were in a butcher shop. Dave had gotten hold of old butcher's refrigerators, which were used to display pairs of sneakers and skateboarding equipment, along with butcher's hooks, which were used to hang T-shirts. Such an original idea!

In 2004, Nike and David Ortiz designed this model, nicknamed the "Bacon," in the colors of that famous pork product, and made to embody the store's concept. Very few pairs were sold at the time, and it can be hard to find your size (especially in good condition). That explains why resale prices were as high as $2,500 (€2,000) for a pair in 2004!

Dave's Quality Meats × Nike Air Max 90 "Bacon"
Release date: 2004, rereleased 03/26/2021 for Air Max Day
Retail price: $120 in 2004, $140 in 2021
Resale price:
2004 Model: $540–$1,600 (€500–€1,500) as of April 2023
2021 Model: $160–$216 (€150–€200) as of April 2023

YOU'LL HAVE TO CLAW FOR THIS LOBSTER!

Concepts × Nike SB Dunk Low "Lobster"

The collaboration between Nike and the Concepts brand, born in Cambridge, Massachusetts, gave us the "Lobster" series, whose release has become something of a tradition! Concepts is one of the leading skate shops that gets a Nike SB (skateboard) account. The store is also famous for its numerous successful collaborations, in particular on the theme of food—such as the famous "TurDUNKen," which is inspired by an American recipe for a turkey that gets stuffed with a duck and a chicken, an innovative Thanksgiving dish!

The Lobster × Nike SB Dunks are the perfect example of pairs that had value even at a time when 95 percent of sneaker addicts were paying no attention to the Nike Dunk. The concept for this Lobster pack is based on the fact that Cambridge, Concepts' city of origin, is famous for its lobster. Hence the shoe's microdotted suede upper, which brings to mind the crustacean's shell. The pairs are delivered with two bands on the toe box (front part of the sneakers), which mimic the rubber bands that are placed on lobsters' claws so you don't wreck your fingers. Also note the liner, which looks like the traditional tablecloths at lobster restaurants.

The Red Lobster came out in 2008, followed by the Blue Lobster and the Yellow Lobster in 2009, for which an F&F (Friends and Family) version was distributed solely to the Concepts team. This is truly a grail item for sneakerheads because production was limited to thirty-six pairs worldwide. The choice of this color is perfectly obvious once you know that you have an approximately one-in-forty-million chance of pulling up a yellow lobster from a Maine fishing trap. The Purple Lobster and Green Lobster came out in 2018, followed by the Orange Lobster in 2022. As of January 2020, all the Lobster × Nike SB Dunk models were sold in striped skateboard boxes. The shoes came in transparent mirrored boxes that mimicked the lobster traps and were often sold in-store, with no internet availability, in an effort to take the packaging on these pairs even further! The 2022 Orange Lobster was part of a collection in tribute to Salvador Dalí and his *Lobster Telephone*, which you can incidentally find on the Exclusive Concept Special Box. A Bearbrick Medicom Toy × Concept Orange Lobster, along with a skateboard designed by Todd Bratrud (who's well known in skateboard collaborations), were sold at the same time.

Concepts × Nike SB Dunk Low "Lobster"

Concepts × Nike SB Dunk Low "Lobster"
Release date:
Red Lobster: 05/31/2008
Blue Lobster: 06/20/2009
Yellow Lobster: 07/27/2009
Purple Lobster: 12/14/2018
Green Lobster: 12/14/2018
Orange Lobster: 12/20/2022

Retail price: $100–$130 (€90 to €130)
Resale price (as of April 2023):
Red Lobster: $2,160–$7,000 (€2,000-€6,500)
Blue Lobster: $2,160–$3,800 (€2,000-€3,500)
Yellow Lobster F&F: up to $43,200 (€40,000)
Purple Lobster: $1,300–$1,800 (€1,200-€1,700)
Green Lobster: $1,080–$2,050 (€1,000-€1,900)
Orange Lobster: $325–$650 (€300–€600)

ICE CREAM MANIA

THE WINNER

Ben & Jerry's × Nike SB Dunk Low "Chunky Dunky" (F&F Special Box)

This pair came straight out of the imagination of the Nike SB team, which very simply wanted to design a cool project with an over-the-top aesthetic. Nike teamed up with the American ice cream company Ben & Jerry's to create this completely eccentric pair, which fits Ben & Jerry's visuals perfectly: green pastures, cows, sun, and blue sky. The shoe has one part that's calfskin with imitation pony and has the distinctive feature of having a Swoosh that's melting—like ice cream in the sun. The pair's name, "Chunky Dunky," also brings to mind a famous ice cream flavor, Chunky Monkey. The pair was released as a limited edition in skate shops with a Nike SB partnership. A few lucky recipients got an F&F version in a special box shaped like an ice cream container.

Ben & Jerry's × Nike SB Dunk Low "Chunky Dunky" (F&F Special Box)
Release date: 05/23/2020
Retail price: $100
Resale price: $1,080–$2,700 (€1,000–€2,500) and $1,620–$4,000 (€1,500–€3,700) for the F&F Special Boxes as of April 2023

URBAN
SNEAKERS
MODELS INSPIRED BY CITIES!

An Incredibly Vast Universe!

This category could be the subject of a book unto itself—that's how many pairs there are on this theme. I'll therefore introduce you to those I feel stand out from the crowd. Please note that I won't mention pairs from football or basketball clubs that are not directly linked to cities, such as the Adidas sneakers in the colors of the British clubs or those Jordans that refer to the NBA teams.

Reebok Instapump Fury "City Pack" 2020

This collection by Reebok gives a nod to four major cities of western Asia: Tokyo, Osaka, Shanghai, and Seoul. These pairs have details such as GPS coordinates on the heel of the soles, maps on the insoles, a compass etched into the pump button on the tongue, and, for the pair in tribute to Seoul, a reminder of the GPS coordinates on the outer upper heel. A Tokyo Pack came out exclusively at Atmos one month earlier, which combined a red Instapump Fury with another black pair, in a limited edition.

Reebok Instapump Fury "City Pack" 2020
Release date: 05/15/2020
Sale price: ¥18,000 ($169)
Resale price: Unknown

Adidas Nite Jogger City Pack

I was lucky enough to take part in the Adidas launch of the Nite Jogger in London in January 2019—so it's a pair that I know well. It was designed for night runners, as the name suggests. It therefore contains numerous components in reflective 3M, which allow you to stay visible in the dark, although this pair is also a great lifestyle shoe.

This truly spot-on pair represents six jet-set capitals and is inspired by the nighttime lights of these big cities. One hip detail: The tongue is covered by a sewn patch that looks like those sticky bands that airlines attach to your bags before flights. Shanghai, Los Angeles, New York, Tokyo, London, and Paris are represented in this excellent pack, which the three-stripe brand meticulously produced.

Adidas Nite Jogger City Pack
Release dates: 03/30/2019 and 04/13/2019
Sale price: $150
Resale price: unknown

Footshop × KangaROOS Ultimate 3 "The City of a Thousand Spires"

Footshop × KangaROOS Ultimate 3 "The City of a Thousand Spires"
Release date: 09/22/2018
Retail price: €270

This shoe was produced as 502 numbered pairs of an Ultimate 3 model, using raw materials hand-assembled at the KangaROOS German factories. The sneaker features the colors of the rooftops of Prague, which is known as "the city of a thousand spires"—hence the name. These sneakers have cutting-edge patterns on the mudguard, which symbolize the Prague spires. A second "reverse" version, which is just as great, came out one year later.

More than a great collaboration, to me this model has a lot of sentimental value. Indeed, in my professional life, I have worked for many years with Footshop, the undisputed leader of the sneaker market and streetwear in the Czech Republic. Over time, I've become friends with Johanna, who is the coordinator for the French market, and Kovkou, the creative director, who has also played a large role in developing Footshop, alongside Peter Hajduček, its founder. I was lucky enough to be invited to Prague for the release party for this pair, which is also known as the "Rooftop," since it's inspired by the Prague rooftops. The event happened to take place on the rooftop of one of the city's old buildings. While I was there, I was invited to visit Johanna and Kovkou, and I was able to admire their personal sneaker collections. What a fantastic memory—getting the opportunity to have encounters like these is such a boon for a sneaker fan!

CHAMPION OF COMMUNICATIONS

Adidas EQT Support 93/17 BVG (Berliner Verkehrsbetriebe)

Now here's a pair that has made its mark on the times . . . I completely loved the concept of this release, which was limited to five hundred pairs and sold exclusively in the famous Overkill boutique in Berlin. For a Berliner using mass transport, this pair was a steal, because in addition to being in the colors of the BVG (Berliner Verkehrsbetriebe), the company that operates the subway, tramway, and bus system for the urban area of Berlin, the pair also served as a citywide ticket for the year 2018. For some, it was even more advantageous to purchase the €500 pair at resale than to get a transit pass! This model incorporates all the city subway tropes: the stained fabric of the seats, a black upper, laces in yellow like the subway cars, and . . . an annual ticket sewn into the tongue! Now's that marketing perfection!

Adidas EQT Support 93/17 BVG (Berliner Verkehrsbetriebe)
Release dates: 01/16/2018 and 03/30/2019
Sale price: €180
Resale price: unknown

STOCKHOLM ADDICT

Sneakersnstuff × Vans OG Classic Slip-On LX "Stockholm"

This pair is a great tribute to the Swedish capital, where SNS (Sneakersnstuff) is headquartered. This is a limited edition inspired by Stockholm, the city that was the birthplace of the famous brand SNS, which has now expanded internationally. Since Stockholm is home to the famous square Sergels torg—nicknamed "Platten" ("the slab") by the city's residents—and this is where the first skaters would come to practice, the model reinvents that strong Vans checkerboard symbol by using the iconic triangle design of the square's pavers. This design fits the first collaboration between SNS and Vans to a T. The pair also contains a premium leather liner; hence the designation LX, for "luxe." The Friends and Family version also came with a limited-edition skateboard (just fifty skateboards were produced).

Sneakersnstuff × Vans OG Classic Slip-On LX « Stockholm »
Release date: 05/09/2015
Sale price: €80

THE ROMAN EMPIRE

The Good Will Out × Diadora
"The Rise and Fall of the Roman Empire" Pack

The German retailer TGWO (The Good Will Out) collaborated with the Italian brand Diadora to pay tribute to the history of the city of Rome and its empire. This pack—which in French was nicknamed "The rise and fall of the Roman empire"—evokes two of its historic emperors: Caligula, for glory, and Nero, for the fall. The Caligula-inspired model is represented by the Diadora V7000. Made of beige suede and pony hair, it has the label TGWO stamped on the tongue, along with a coin with Caligula's face etched onto the heels. As for the Nero-inspired model, it's represented by a red Diadora S8000, also made of suede and pony hair, with an etched coin of Nero on the heels. This pack, which was released as a limited edition, was sold via raffle exclusively at TGWO.

The Good Will Out × Diadora "The Rise and Fall of the Roman Empire" Pack
Release date: 06/17/2017
Sale price: €190
Resale price: unknown

THE ROMANE EMPIRE, AGAIN

The Good Will Out × Diadora "N9000 SPQR" Pack

One month after "The Rise and Fall," the folks at German brand TGWO once again teamed up with Diadora to pay tribute to the splendor of the Roman Empire, with The Good Will Out × Diadora N9000 SPQR model. The inscription "SPQR" that you find on the heel and on one of the pennants covering the laces is an abbreviation for Senatus Populusque Romanus, the motto of the Roman Republic and later of the Roman Empire, which means "The Senate and the Roman People." These four letters represented the Roman political power and still today are the symbol for the city of Rome. The pair is red and gold, the colors of the famous high-ranking centurions, the primus pilus. Just 447 pairs were available for sale.

The Good Will Out × Diadora "N9000 SPQR" Pack
Release date: 07/08/2017
Sale price: €190
Resale price: $270 (€250) as of March 2023

VENICE AMORE

BAIT × Diadora N9000 "Notti Veneziane"

This is the first collaboration between the quintessential Californian brand BAIT and Diadora. There will be many others. As its name suggests, the "Notti Veneziane" is inspired by Venetian nights: textured faux snakeskin made from violet premium Italian leather, "BAIT" stamped in gold letters inside and on the tongue, and, lastly a speckled rubber sole that supports the whole. The pair is usually sold with several pairs of original laces in leather and velvet.

The N9000 is a running shoe from 1990 that is now one of Diadora's most popular models. This pair has no particular backstory, but it is a really nice pair of sneakers—super classy, just like Venice.

BAIT × Diadora N9000 "Notti Veneziane"
Release date: 02/13/2016
Sale price: $220

BROOKLYN ADDICT

Sophia Chang × Puma Disc Brooklynite Collection

In 2014, New York designer and illustrator Sophia Chang created Brooklynite, a collection in collaboration with Puma in homage to Brooklyn nights. The pack consists of three pairs of Puma Disc Blaze sneakers: one black, one white, and one blue—colors inspired by the facades of city buildings as seen from Brooklyn at night. The detail that I like the most is the golden seal on the heel that's inscribed with the words "Believe the hype," along with a picture of the Brooklyn Bridge.

Sophia Chang × Puma Disc Brooklynite Collection
Release dates: August and September 2014
Sale price: €140 and €150

NEW BALANCE'S
INCREDIBLE CITIES

New Balance has a large catalog of pairs that pay tribute to cities, mainly in connection with major marathons. The brand has also released several Flimby anniversary packs, in reference to New Balance's flagship factory in England—a true gauge of excellence for collectors. When the words "Made in England" are embroidered on the tongue, you know it's a high-quality pair!

Flimby pack by Hanon, fortieth anniversary

Flimby pack, thirty-fifth anniversary

Overkill × New Balance
"Berlin—City of Values" Pack

The Berliners at the Overkill boutique have paid tribute to their city's electronica culture with two pairs: a gray/pastel M1500 and a black M1503, representing the night and day, respectively. Three words are embroidered on the tongues: "Equality, Unity, Diversity," a motto that's embodied by a city that hosts events such as the Love Parade, Gay Pride, and, of course, numerous electronica nights. For the release of this pack, the Overkill teams organized an outdoor rave in the neighborhood of the club Else, which is truly the epicenter of the Berlin electronica scene. This pack was sold exclusively at Overkill, as a limited edition.

Overkill' × New Balance "Berlin—City of Values" Pack
Release date: 06/22/2019
Sale price: €170

Shoe Gallery × New Balance MT580
"Tour de Miami"

This pair, which slipped completely under the radar, is a true personal favorite. It's now possible to find this magnificent model at a price close to the original one, and even under retail price with a little luck. This shoe was created in collaboration with Shoe Gallery, a Miami retailer that wanted to pay tribute to the local cycling race, the Tour de Miami, which was named in reference to the Tour de France. The blue nubuck represents the Miami sky, while the touch of charcoal symbolizes the bikes. A picture of the race route is also printed on the insole.

Shoe Gallery × New Balance MT580 "Tour de Miami"

Release date: 11/22/2014
Sale price: $160
The New Balance 580 is from 1995.

NIKE CITY

Let's move on to Nike, which has numerous pairs in the colors of major cities. I've counted hundreds of models and "City" packs at the brand with the Swoosh, so I'm going to focus on a few models that are really quintessential and iconic.

First of all, I'd like to mention some models and packs that I really love: the Nike Air Max 1 "London & Amsterdam" City Pack of 2020, which boasts premium materials and outstanding details such as a map of the Amsterdam canals on the heel, or even the Nike Air Max BW City Pack of 2021, which contains four pairs: Los Angeles, Beijing, Lyon, and Rotterdam, the city where I was born. The City Pack Tour for the Air Jordan Xs, which came out in 2016 and was inspired by a Jordan × City Pack from 1995, is particularly well executed. It contains eight pairs in all: New York, Paris, Chicago, Los Angeles, Shanghai, Rio, London, and Charlotte. Lastly, the Nike Air Max Plus "City Special—Atlanta" deserves a special mention. The women's version in pink from that City Special pack is truly incredible.

Nike Air Max 1 "London & Amsterdam" City Pack, London model

Nike Air Max Plus City "Special Atlanta"

Air Jordan × City Pack Tour, Rio model

Air Jordan × City Pack Tour, Paris model

Nike Air Max 1 "London & Amsterdam" City Pack, Amsterdam model

Nike Air Max BW City Pack

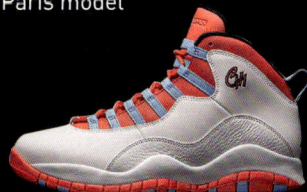

Air Jordan × City Pack Tour, Chicago model

Fragment Design × Nike Dunk High City Pack

In 2010, the famous label Fragment Design by Hiroshi Fujiwara, still not very well known to the general public at that time, collaborated with Nike on this City Pack, an urban collection containing three pairs of Nike Dunk Highs in mismatched colors.

The number of pairs produced remains unknown, although the Beijing model in reversed shades of somber black and purple on the left and right feet is the least rare of the three. The history of this model is not very well known. Incidentally, it was rereleased in 2021 and went completely unnoticed, to the point that it ended up in the Nike Factory Stores (outlets), which proves it's possible to find hidden gems when you know what to look for.

The yellow and pink shades of the London model were directly inspired by the cover to *Never Mind the Bollocks, Here's the Sex Pistols*, a punk album by the Sex Pistols that came out in 1977. The London punk movement greatly influenced fashion in Japan, specifically in the Harajuku neighborhood of Tokyo. Since Hiroshi Fujiwara was himself a musician, the choice of this colorway makes perfect sense!

Lastly, the Chicago model is the rarest of the three, since only around a hundred pairs were produced. The Chicago was created for Fragment Design by Sk8thing, co-creator of the brand Cav Empt and the graphic designer and artist behind major brands in the Harajuku neighborhood, such as Bape, WTAPS, and even Neighborhood, as well as for international brands such as BBC Ice Cream, which is Pharrell Williams's brand. While the Beijing and London models of the shoes featured reversed colors on the left and right feet, the colors on the Chicago pair were completely different for each foot! But why? It was a wink to the Japanese fashion at that time: The Nike Dunk worked really well in the land of the rising sun, and Japanese fans of this model loved to wear two different colors on their feet, with the laces tied very tight all the way up. As for the range of red, white, and black on this pair, it refers to Michael Jordan's Jordan 1 OG "Chicago" sneakers and highlights the significant resemblance between the Jordan 1 and the Nike Dunk, two models that were designed by the late Peter Moore and both released in 1985.

Fragment Design × Nike Dunk High City Pack

Release date: 12/18/2010
Sale price: $90
Beijing resale price: $325–$975 (€300–€900) as of April 2023
London resale price: $2,160–$4,860 (€2,000–€4,500) as of April 2023
Chicago resale price: $4,320–$8,640 (€4,000–€8,000) as of April 2023

Nike SB Dunk High Pro "Statue of Liberty"

The Nike SB Dunk High Pro "Statue of Liberty" is a very special model, specifically thanks to its manufacture and a very wise choice of finishes. The pair is in the same color as New York's iconic Statue of Liberty, whose face appears on the tongue and insole. The icing on the cake is the seagrass shade, which covers another, reddish-brown color. Therefore, as the pair gets used, it appears to oxidize just like the copper on the Statue of Liberty! This is certainly one of the best Nike SB Dunks of 2011, which came out as a "QS" (Quickstrike) limited edition.

Nike SB Dunk High Pro "Statue of Liberty"

Release date: 03/05/2011
Sale price: $130
Resale price: $430–$864 (€400–€800) as of April 2023

DID YOU KNOW?

Sneaker addicts classify the best models according to how easily they can be purchased.

- Therefore, a limited-edition pair that can nonetheless be snatched up ("copped") if you have the means is referred to as "heat," meaning a sneaker that is very rare or cool.

- Then there are the "grails," such as the AM1 "Chlorophyll."

- Lastly, there are the "holy grails," such as the "Amsterdams" or even the legendary "Albert Heijn" model. You can find hundreds of photos of people wearing this model on social media. Once you know that only twenty-four pairs have been distributed to friends of the artist, it's easy to figure out that they can't all be originals. Happily, it's pretty easy to determine if pairs that are nearly twenty years old are counterfeit.

Nike Air Max 1 "Albert Heijn" F&F

Just twenty-four pairs of this model were officially distributed to friends of the artist Piet Janssen, owner of Parra. It features the design that was intended to feature the colors of Albert Heijn supermarket bags (see following page for the incredible story behind the Parra × Nike Air Max 1 "AMS").

Nike Air Max 1 "Albert Heijn" F&F

Release date: pair not sold
Resale price: Since this pair is nearly impossible to find, it's very difficult to estimate its price.

Parra × Nike Air Max 1 "AMS" (Amsterdam)

This pair is indisputably my favorite in the streetwear category, even though other models that were in higher demand in 2023 are worth more.

The Nike Air Max 1 "AMS," referring to Amsterdam, is the result of an unforeseen circumstance. Originally, the designer Parra was supposed to collaborate with Nike and work off the blue, yellow, and orange bags from the Dutch supermarket chain Albert Heijn. The model was finalized and about to go into production when Albert Heijn changed the color of its bags. What to do? It was such a disappointment and so frustrating to see the entire project fall apart at the last minute! Something had to be done, and Piet Janssen, the thoughtful owner of Parra, knew exactly what, masterfully transforming his model, which had initially been geared toward an industrial pop art theme, into a pair of sneakers that became the talk of the town. The Nike Air Max 1 "Amsterdam," also dubbed "Red Light District," was a nod to Amsterdam's notorious red-light district, where scantily clad prostitutes appear under blue and pink neon signs behind the dark, red-curtained glass windows of Dutch brick row houses (to which the official colorway also alludes). This pair by Parra features mesh, leather, and suede on the outer mudguard protecting the shoe and is stamped with the words "Amsterdam King" on the heels, along with a crown on the tongue.

Parra × Nike Air Max 1 "AMS" (Amsterdam)

Release date: 08/01/2005
Sale price: $110
Resale price: Since very few pairs are available, prices are at sellers' discretion and depend on buyers' offers. The rare pairs available were sold for $5,400 (€5,000) and $27,000 (€25,000) in 2023.

Nike SB Dunk Low Pro City Pack

This SB Dunk pack dating back to the early aughts comes in four different styles, each corresponding to an iconic city: Paris, Tokyo, London, and New York. We'll discuss each of them with Jusb13, who's an authority on the model.

JUSB13: Honestly, this pair leaves me speechless. . . . As you reminded us, it was sold in three Parisian shops: Opium, Colette, and Starcow. At the time, another little store in Paris, Tokyoïte (which has since closed), had the good sense to buy the few available pairs. In less than three weeks, the price went from €350 to €850 (about $413 to $1,003). What a shame; I should have bought all of them! It's an absolute grail sneaker—well, it's my absolute grail at least. What more can I say?

Nike SB Dunk Low Pro "Paris"

This is a pair that was originally supposed to be sold at the exhibition *White Dunk: Evolution of an Icon* at the Palais de Tokyo in 2003 in Paris. However, its release had to be pushed back, and the exhibition was never held. This model was ultimately sold at certain, carefully selected Paris stores, such as Colette and Opium. Symbolizing Paris and France required selecting a famous Parisian artist. This pair features a patchwork of different works by the painter Bernard Buffet, who died in 1999 (i.e., three years earlier). These are now the rarest pair of Nike SB Dunks around—and consequently one of the most expensive pairs of sneakers in the world.

Jusb13 and I in July 2021, pictured with the Nike SB collections amassed by Ju and Elie Costa, two of the biggest collectors of this model in Europe.

Nike SB Dunk Low Pro "Paris"

Release date: March 2002
Retail price: $60
Resale price: $20,500–$61,500 (€19,000–€57,000) as of 2023
Limited to 202 pairs worldwide

JUSB13: Here's one of the hardest pairs to find. As far as I recall, I've only ever encountered one or two people who had it in my size. I'm not a big fan of this colorway because it shows every speck of dirt.

Nike SB Dunk Low Pro "Tokyo"

This is clearly the most discreet sneaker of the pack, and with good reason: That's the whole point of its design. It's a pair that aims to be the very essence of the Nike SB Dunk, with an upper made solely of muslin, which is a completely pure and untreated fabric. The design pushes simplicity so far that there isn't even a Nike logo on the heel patch or tongue. It's really a pair for connoisseurs.

Nike SB Dunk Lo Pro "Tokyo"

Release date: January 2004
Retail price: $60
Resale price: $9,700–$14,000 (€9,000–€13,000) as of 2023
Limited edition of 202 pairs worldwide

Nike SB Dunk Low Pro "London"

This pair was also intended to be sold during the exhibition *White Dunk: Evolution of an Icon*. The sneakers were ultimately sold exclusively at Footpatrol in London. They're light gray and dark gray suede, in homage to the smoky look we associate with London (the city's been known as "the Old Smoke" since the 1950s). This pair also features an illustration of a branch of the Thames embroidered on the outer heel.

Nike SB Dunk Low Pro "London"

Release date: January 2004
Retail price: $60
Resale price: $16,200–$23,700 (€15,000–€22,000) as of 2023
Limited edition of 202 pairs worldwide

JUSB13: I'm really feeling that little gray-blue squiggle. On a sidenote, I was on the hunt for this pair for years, and then I found them late one night on eBay.com. After discussing it with the seller, I realized that he lived in Paris, five minutes from my apartment. It was definitely a sign!

Nike SB Dunk Low Pro "NYC Pigeon"

This pair is also known as the "Riot" because on the day of its release, February 22, 2005, the mood in front of the Reed Space store in lower Manhattan was so charged that the police had to intervene to calm everyone down. The event made the front page of the *New York Post* the next day, with the title "Sneaker Frenzy" in caps. This has remained one of the most important moments in sneaker history, even though it was not the first time there was such an uproar. The release of the Air Jordan XI Concord in 2000 in New York, the cradle of sneaker culture, had also made the front page of the *Post*.

Jeff Staple was behind the design of the "NYC Pigeon." He's the founder of the Staple Design visual communications agency, which has been around since 1997. Staple is now also a brand whose logo is a pigeon.

Since the pigeon is the most common animal in New York City, it's become something of a symbol. Hence the pigeon on the heel of this pair of shoes and the gray color, which is close to the color of the bird.

While the "Paris" SB is the most expensive, the "Pigeon Riot" is the most popular. Jeff Staple once again collaborated in late 2017 and early 2019 on two new models of the Nike SB Dunk Low "Pigeon," including the "Panda Pigeon" in 2019, which had the particular feature of depicting the front page of the *New York Post* underneath the transparent outsole.

Nike SB Dunk Low Pro "NYC Pigeon"

Release date: February 22, 2005
Retail price: $200
Resale price: $27,000–$43,200 (€25,000–€40,000) as of 2023
Limited edition of 202 pairs worldwide

JUSB13: This is no doubt the second nicest pair in the pack. All sneakerheads want to own the shoe that set off one of the first sneaker fan skirmishes on the day of its release. Generally speaking, all of Jeff Staple's collaborations (including three for Nike SB), even with brands other than Nike, are well made. I really love the details in the third collaboration, the "Pigeon Panda," but am a little less keen on the "Black Pigeon," which in my opinion does not have much appeal.

SNEAKERS AND HIP-HOP: THE PERFECT PAIR

HIT SONGS AND SNEAKERS

A COLLABORATION FOR EVERY RAPPER!

Surely one of the most important parts of this book is the cultural connection between the rap world and sneakers. The number of sneakers that are the result of rapper collaborations is as hard to measure as the number of rappers who mention sneakers in their songs! The latter range from Nelly's classic "Air Force Ones" (featuring Kyjuan, Ali, and Murphy Lee) to Run-DMC and "My Adidas," plus more recent songs such as the one from the rapper UK Dave, featuring Stormzy, which begins with the words "Jordan 4 or Jordan 1," and songs from French rappers such as Rim-K, who gave us the classic "Air Max" (featuring Ninho). All rappers, or nearly all, want their own pair of sneakers. It all comes from the street—it's exactly the kind of thing that speaks to us, because we grew up with sneakers on our feet.

I could write a whole book about rap and sneakers (and, who knows, maybe I'll do it someday), but here I'm going to have to focus and distill everything down to the essential—with a dash of what I personally love. There are nevertheless a few pairs that I would absolutely love to mention, such as the collabs from Cardi B and Kendrick Lamar at Reebok, and other pairs that have made their mark on their generation, like 50 Cent's G-Units, also with Reebok. Few people know this, but rapper Snoop Dogg has several pretty cool pairs with Adidas. The three-stripe brand has also worked extensively with rappers such as Pusha T, Joey Bada$$, Stormzy, Kid Cudi, A$AP Ferg, 2 Chainz, and Action Bronson, who did the Ultraboost F&Fs. . . . It's nothing new at Adidas, which had already released the Def Jam × Adidas "25th Anniversary Collection" in 2009, as well as pairs for Method Man and Redman, Young Jeezy, and Ghostface, plus the pairs done for the label and others. Dave East recently got his own pair with Diadora, and Lil Wayne has had several models with a very original design at Supra, as has A$AP Rocky at Vans and Tyler The Creator and even Wiz Khalifa at Converse. . . . But honestly, the list is way too long!

The rapper Raekwon

DIADORA AND RAEKWON

Packer Shoes × Raekwon × Diadora N9000 "Purple Tape"

Now here's a legendary collaboration! It celebrated the twentieth anniversary of the release of *Only Built 4 Cuban Linx*, the first studio album from Raekwon, the great rapper from the famous group Wu-Tang Clan. It was a collaboration with the shop Packer Shoes in New York. The shoe was called "Purple Tape" because it featured the color of that album's purple cassette tape. Other details also pointed to cassettes: the famous Parental Advisory logo, the numbers 1 and 2 on the heels to symbolize both sides of a tape, and a "1995" embroidered in place of the usual "N9000." The pair was released exclusively at SOB's in New York, along with special packaging and a memorable show from the super MC Raekwon.

Packer Shoes × Raekwon × Diadora N9000 "Purple Tape"

Release date: 08/20/2015
Retail price: $200
Resale price: $648–$864 (€600–€800) as of 2023

Packer × Raekwon × Diadora N9000 "Cuban Linx"

Five years after "Purple Tape" N9000, the "Cuban Linx" came out in December 2020 to celebrate the twenty-fifth anniversary of Raekwon The Chef's legendary first studio album, *Only Built 4 Cuban Linx*.

The "Purple Tape" sneakers were made in the colors of that album's audio cassette, while this pair was done in the colors of the CD version. The album came out on August 1, 1995, and rose to number two on the Top R&B/Hip-Hop Albums and to number four on the 2008 Billboard list. It went gold on October 2, 1995.

The shoe still gives a few nods to "Purple Tape," notably in the sneaker's mauve "1 and 2" insoles (sides A and B) and the packaging (a mauve plastic pouch). The mention "1995" is on the heel, and "Packer, Raekwon, Diadora N9000" is indicated on the patch of the tongue, in the fashion of the "Parental Advisory" logo. The model features pony hair, perforated leather, faux ostrich skin–textured leather, suede, and mesh. It's fair to say that this collection is really well made! Incidentally, the shoe also celebrates the thirtieth anniversary of the classic Diadora N9000. To conclude, this pair was originally a prototype for the release of the "Purple Tape" shoe—only the chef had a pair of them in 2015. The limited-edition shoe was released exclusively at Packer Shoes and on its website.

Diadora and Raekwon collaborated on three additional pairs, but, in my opinion, these two pairs pack the biggest punch.

Packer × Raekwon × Diadora N9000 "Cuban Linx"

Release date: 12/23/2020
Retail price: $250
Resale Price: $205–$460 (€200–€450) as of July 2022

NEW BALANCE'S EXPLOSIVE PALETTE

Action Bronson × New Balance 990V6 Made in USA "Baklava"

One of my favorite rappers, Action Bronson (a.k.a. Bam Bam Baklava), who comes to us from Queens and is also the star of the program *F*ck, That's Delicious*, finally did his own "real" collaboration with Boston giant New Balance, which is all the rage. The brand's creative director for the United States, Teddy Santis, is also the creator of the excellent New York brand Aimé Leon Dore (ALD). If I'm very insistent here, it's because Action Bronson took part in a shoot for ALD's FW21 collection two years earlier, and I love to think that this is where the relationship between Teddy Santis and Action Bronson began. This Baklava 990V6 is yet another design born from a collaboration. It's the first of a series of 990V6 Baklavas, and whatever other models are still to come (why not?). The color palette used on this pair (Pixel Green / Dazzling Blue) is (to say the least) original and has a casual vibe. The sneakers are (naturally) stamped "Baklava" on the insoles and tongue patch and sit atop a FuelCell technology sole, which ensures a comfortable, lightweight fit. I think it's a successful pair that fits the rapper to a T.

Action Bronson × New Balance 990V6 Made in USA "Lapis Lazuli"

The second pair from Action Bronson, the great Queens chef and rapper, is identical to the Baklavas, except for the colorway. The "Lapis Lazuli" sneakers feature colors evoking those of the stone. A third pair in yellow is also set for release, along with a Baklava × New Balance capsule collection of clothing.

Action Bronson × New Balance 990V6 Made in USA "Baklava"
Release date: 04/25/2023
Retail price: $220
Resale price: $216–$648 (€200–€600) as of April 2023

Action Bronson × New Balance 990V6 Made in USA "Lapis Lazuli"
Release date: 05/06/2023
Retail price: $220
Resale price: $390 (€360) on average as of July 2023

ASICS, LEATHER, AND LUXURY

Extra Butter × Ghostface Killah × Asics Gel Lyte MT "Pretty Toney"

Even though it's not legendary Wu-Tang rapper Ghostface Killah's first collaboration, this shoe is without a doubt a wonder. One of the most popular shops in New York City, Extra Butter, partnered with Ghostface Killah and Asics to bring us a superb Gel Lyte MT in the colors of the leather jacket that Ghostface wore in a comedy miniseries that aired on MTV back in the day. In the series, the rapper embodied one of his alter egos, Pretty Toney. A limited edition was first released at ComplexCon, then at the Extra Butter boutique. A New Era collaboration accompanied the release. The pair is stamped "GFK" alongside the tongue closure; straps, snaps, and several textured premium leathers (quilted, ostrich skin, etc.) top the shoe off in luxurious fashion.

Extra Butter × Ghostface Killah × Asics Gel Lyte MT "Pretty Toney"

Release date: 11/04/2017
Retail price: $180
Resale price: $325 (€300) as of April 2023

UNDER ARMOR GOES TO HARLEM

A$AP Rocky "AWGE" × Under Armor SRLo

In 2017, A$AP Rocky, the superstar, member, and headliner of A$AP Mob, signed a contract with Under Armor with the aim of boosting the brand's lifestyle line. One year and a lot of suspense later, the "AWGE" × Under Armor SRLo (Skate, Rave, Lo) was finally unveiled, with a release scheduled for September 14. Two colorways (black/black and black/blue) were sold in a limited edition of 250 pairs, each during a skate rave at a Harlem pop-up store. A$AP's choice of shoe (which was full-on inspired by nineties' skate shoes and, more specifically, the Osiris D3) was surprising to some. The artist really knew how to mix the trends of 2018, when Nike Dunks were all the rage thanks to Virgil Abloh and luxury brands were going all in for the "dad shoe" design with the futuristic trends at Triple S. You could say it was a wise choice, but although five hundred pairs were of course sold in a snap in Harlem, the collaboration between A$AP Rocky and Under Armor unfortunately did not go any further. . . . Word had it that the artist was too disloyal to the brand with which he'd signed. Yet, they'd done the work, and this story makes the pair even more interesting because it looks like there won't be any others. In terms of details, the SRLos have "AWGE" stamped on the outsole (the design firm founded by A$AP Rocky); there is also a clear circle with a "crash test" logo on the arch of the foot, which is also the artist's visual signature that you can find on various A$AP Rocky collaborations, such as the one he did with Nigo's Human Made. The individual bags and boxes were designed in the same "crash test" spirit and are truly unique.

A$AP Rocky "AWGE" × Under Armor SRLo
Release date: 09/14/2018
Retail price: $250
Resale price: $325–$810 (€300–€750) as of April 2023

VERSACE AND 2CHAINZ, A LUXURY COLLABORATION!

2 Chainz × Versace Chain Reaction

At a time when "true" sneaker addicts were still looking down on so-called luxury sneakers, the Versace Chain Reaction came to set the record straight with its successful design, as extravagant as it was unique. Rapper 2 Chainz, who was accustomed to opulent, luxurious styles, signed a deal with the similarly opulent and luxurious brand Versace—and nothing against the brand, but sneakers were not really the niche you'd expect from it! Seen for the first time at the Versace runway show during the 2018 Milan Fashion Week, the Chain Reaction very quickly made the rounds on sneaker blogs and websites and, as its name predicted, triggered a lot of reactions, both good and bad. The design was at the cutting edge of Versace's baroque rococo style, modernized by the rapper and his signature style of always wearing two chains (2 Chainz), as well as by of-the-moment designer Salehe Bembury. I'll point out that while Salehe Bembury was beginning to make a name for himself in fashion and design, it was indeed thanks to Chain Reaction that he became known to a larger audience. Versace still makes the Chain Reaction, and it has become a full-fledged model, available in numerous colorways. Of course, what makes this model work its charm, in addition to the ultra-clean details, is clearly the sole, which mimics the links of a chain. The workmanship is incredible—kudos to 2 Chainz and Salehe Bembury.

The Chain Reaction, pictured here in green, is one of my favorite models. It was a collaboration with the renowned sneaker shop Concepts, which did its take on the patterns and color of the famous Versace dress that Jennifer Lopez wore to the 2000 Grammy Awards.

2 Chainz × Versace Chain Reaction

Release date: March 2018
Retail price: $995–$1,350, depending on materials
Resale price: Unknown

REEBOK'S HIGH-IMPACT COLLABORATIONS

Curren$y × Reebok Question Mid "Jet Life"

Since Curren$y is one of my favorite artists, I simply could not pass up this collaboration, which centered on the theme of cars, the rapper's passion. This model was christened "Jet Life," after Curren$y's label. The pair contains numerous incredibly delicate and stylish details with a lowrider aesthetic, and it comes in packaging shaped like a lowrider trunk. The words "Jet Life" are stamped on the heels, and the tongue has been doubled up for the occasion. The pair was released as a limited edition, exclusively at Sneaker Politics in Louisiana, Curren$y's home state.

Curren$y × Reebok Question Mid "Jet Life"
Release date: 03/05/2018
Retail price: $170
Resale price: $216–$430 (€200–€400) as of April 2023

Cam'ron × Reebok Question Mid

It wasn't the first time that the famous rapper from the Diplomats collaborated with Reebok—for example, he'd already done the Reebok Ventilator "Purple Haze." Incidentally, Cam'ron found the inspiration to create this violet camo sneaker by once again focusing on his *Purple Haze* album. Details like the inscribed "Dipset" on the tongue and the flip phone on the silver button of the heel topped off this model, which combined the spirit of the shoe with the rapper's aesthetic.

The hip-hop collective the Diplomats, composed of Cam'ron, Jim Jones, Freekey Zekey, and Juelz Santana, was one of the most influential groups in rap and hip-hop culture during the 1990s and first decade of the 2000s.

Cam'ron × Reebok Question Mid
Release date: 08/20/2018
Retail price: $200
Resale price: Unknown

Swizz Beatz × Reebok Kamikaze III

In the early aughts, rapper and producer Swizz Beatz was really a driving force for Reebok's lifestyle line. Thanks to him, there was a true "Kamikaze" period. Alas, it ended, no doubt due to the production of too many colorways. Indeed, the rarity of a model largely contributes to the hype and, thus, to demand. Swizz Beatz nevertheless revisited this classic pair for his version III in 2011. Personally, I still have very good memories of this model, which I wore for a really long time. I was particularly drawn to the big Hexalite windows on the sides of the shoe, which later turned up on the Reebok "Sermon."

In June 2011, two new colorways were released: Gray / Steel / Sonic Green and Black / White / Blazing Orange. These models were released exclusively at select shops in eleven major American cities.

Swizz Beatz × Reebok Kamikaze III
Release date: 06/10/2011
Retail price: $100
Resale price: Unknown

Reebok S. Carter

In 2003, Reebok made a really good move when it signed hip-hop superstars Jay-Z (Shawn Corey Carter), for the "S. Carter Collection by RBK," and 50 Cent, for the "G-Unit by RBK." Even though Run-DMC had paved the way with Adidas in 1986, signing a $1 million contract, collaborations with rappers were not yet commonplace in 2003—far from it. Sales of the first Reebok S. Carters were very successful in the United States. Ten thousand pairs were sold for $100 each, primarily at Foot Locker. The sneakers came with a CD of previously unreleased music by Jay-Z. The ten thousand pairs flew off the shelves in a week, which, at the time, was considered the fastest sale of shoes in history. In this respect, we must admit that times have changed significantly since then! Despite this success, the following S. Carter collections did not reach record sales, and 50 Cent quickly surpassed Jay-Z and his S. Carters with the Reebok G-Unit. Jay-Z's contract with Reebok had a four-year term, and this collaboration contributed to an 11 percent increase in the sale of sneakers—Reebok's stock rose 20 percent!

The S. Carter design is directly inspired by a Gucci shoe, the "Tennis Gucci 84," the preferred pair of New York dealers in the 1980s! There is a blatant resemblance.

Reebok S. Carter

Release date: 04/18/2003
Retail price: $100
Resale price: Unknown

Tennis Gucci 84

ADIDAS
CHANGES THE GAME

In the mid-1980s, propelling Adidas to center stage was a music group from New York: Run-DMC. Composed of Joseph Simmons (Rev Run), Jason Mizell (Jam Master Jay), and Darryl McDaniels (DMC), the group broke the codes of hip-hop with its street style. Their fedoras, Cazal glasses, gold chains, tracksuits, and pairs of laceless Superstars were a nod to youths held in police custody. They looked very different from the usual hip-hop style icons—for example, rapper and DJ Grandmaster Flash wore a leather Perfecto and cowboy boots.

In 1986, the group released the album *Raising Hell*, on which "My Adidas" appears. The song pays tribute to the famous German brand. On a sidenote, Run-DMC had already contacted Adidas for a collaboration, but since the German business was used to working only with athletes, it had refused to partner with the musical group.

Later that year the group gave a concert at Madison Square Garden, the legendary New York venue. Def Jam and Run-DMC invited the Adidas representatives that night. They watched something happen that was unprecedented for an athletic brand. With the first notes of the song "My Adidas," people in the audience began to brandish their pairs of Adidas and Superstars. It was truly a show of strength from the group!

A few days later the group went from "seeker" to "sought." Adidas had realized Run-DMC's impact on American youths. The German firm went on to sign a $1 million contract with the group, which became the first non-athlete ambassadors of an athletic brand. The impact of signing Run-DMC was so big that in six months' time, Adidas' sales shot up 30 percent.

The Adidas Superstar is the symbol of the birth of lifestyle fashion. Even though other models were already beginning to turn up on the street, the Superstar truly ushered in the appeal of the lifestyle concept at brands. From then on, athletic shoes were no longer reserved for just sports and athletes: They could be worn on the street by anyone. Sneakers thus became a fashion phenomenon through a lever other than sports.

As of 2020, the Superstar was still being sold. The pair has slightly evolved over the years but still contains certain unique features. The shoe is immediately recognizable, above all thanks to the digit-protecting "shell toe."

The Superstar has been reinterpreted numerous times. In 2011, a pair of Superstar Run-DMCs came out, followed by other versions in the group's likeness. Pharrell Williams, who also signed with Adidas, has worked on the Superstar. In 2019 and 2020, Adidas collaborated with the luxury brand Prada to create a limited, numbered version in ultra-premium Italian leather. The Superstar has definitively become one of the all-time great sneakers!

PHARRELL WILLIAMS, FROM BAPE TO LOUIS VUITTON

An iconic character in today's fashion world, Pharrell Williams, the man who never ages, was declared a worthy successor to Virgil Abloh as creative director of Louis Vuitton menswear. A successor, sure, although the leader of the N.E.R.D. group was already a mentor for great designers such as Virgil Abloh. Williams, who turned fifty in 2023, is far from being on his first collaboration, and in June 2016 he received a Fashion Icon Award, handed to him by Kanye West. See below for a broad outline of his résumé.

2001–02: Meeting between Pharrell and Nigo in Japan (Bape).

2003: Pharrell and his friend Nigo, for whom Pharrell had already collaborated with Bape, codesigned the Billionaire Boys Club & Ice Cream brand, which—just like Bape—would have an enormous influence on, first, the urban world and, much later, on all of fashion.

2003, cont.: Release of the "Ice Cream" Board Flip by Pharrell sneakers.

2004: Release of the Reebok × Ice Cream "Flavor."

N.E.R.D., Pharrell's group, volunteered to do a now-legendary collaboration on a Nike Dunk High.

2005: Millionaire collection at Louis Vuitton with his friend Nigo (Bape / Human Made). The Millionaire sunglasses are now a must-have at LV. Virgil Abloh had moreover already revamped and featured them.

2006: Release of the Pharrell × Bape Road STA & N.E.R.D. × Bape STA.

2008: Exhibition of furniture designed by Pharrell Williams at the Perrotin gallery.

2011: Release of Domeau & Pérès × Pharrell Williams "Brooklyn Bike": a twelve-bike limited edition later displayed at our (may it rest in peace) fashion temple Collette, where Pharrell was a regular.

2013: Pharrell Williams designed a collection of four sunglasses for Moncler.

2014: Pharrell Williams collaborated with UNIQLO UT on a capsule collection of T-shirts, along with Nigo for DA.

Pharrell Williams participated, alongside his wife and Takashi Murakami, in the exhibition "G I R L" at the Perrotin gallery, for the release of his eponymous album.

Pharrell Williams signed a long-term contract with Adidas.

Pharrell Williams released a collection titled "RAW for the Oceans" with the brand G-Star Raw. The collection of clothing was made using plastic bottle waste recovered from the ocean.

Pharrell Williams released a capsule collection in collaboration with Colette.

2015: New "RAW for the Oceans" collection with the brand G-Star Raw.

Billionaire Boys Club teamed up with Timberland to design the "Bee Line" collection, which was declared best collaboration of the year by Footwear News.

Pharrell Williams collaborated with Chanel and Karl Lagerfeld on a capsule collection of clothing.

Start of the collaborations with Adidas.

2019: Reebok and Ice Cream, who were on bad terms due to defects on certain pairs, reconciled and released new collaborations.

Pharrell Williams and Nigo collaborated once again on a collection from Adidas × Human Made (Nigo's new brand).

2023: In February, the *Wall Street Journal* and *Le Figaro* announced the appointment of Pharrell Williams as creative director of menswear at Louis Vuitton.

Pharrell Williams and Moncler Genius announced "The Art of Terrain" collaboration by Pharrell.

Ice Cream × Reebok "Flavor"

In 2004, Ice Cream collaborated with Reebok and released three pairs of Flavors in special boxes that looked like cartons of ice cream. Each pair contained visual touches that were characteristic of the brand, such as diamonds and dollars. Unfortunately, this collaboration did not last, because, shortly after, Pharrell Williams sued Reebok due to defects on the pairs. However, in 2015 the two made peace, and Ice Cream again collaborated with Reebok (which still belonged to the Adidas group) on rereleases of the Question MID and other sneakers, while Pharrell also simultaneously collaborated with Adidas.

Ice Cream Board Flip by Pharrell

- Release date: 2003
- Retail price: $79.99
- Resale price: Unknown

Ice Cream × Reebok "Flavor"

In 2004, Ice Cream collaborated with Reebok and released three pairs of Flavors in special boxes that looked like cartons of ice cream. Each pair contained visual touches that were characteristic of the brand, such as diamonds and dollars. Unfortunately, this collaboration did not last, because, shortly after, Pharrell Williams sued Reebok due to defects on the pairs. However, in 2015 the two made peace, and Ice Cream again collaborated with Reebok (which still belonged to the Adidas group) on rereleases of the Question MID and other sneakers, while Pharrell also simultaneously collaborated with Adidas.

Ice Cream × Reebok "Flavor"

Release date: August 2004
Retail price: Unknown
Resale price: Unknown

N.E.R.D. × Nike Dunk High

This exceptional pair was released as part of the program known as the "Nike's Artist Series," thanks to which we were able to see the name Stash on an Am BW and Futura on a Blazer in 2003, and, in 2004, a Nike Rift by Halle Berry, Eminem's Air Burst, and even an "Espo" edition (which was, unfortunately, abandoned), along with a Nike Air Force 2 Low created by graffiti artist Stephen Powers. The limited edition was capped at 1,050 numbered pairs. The finely textured black leather had the look of iguana or snakeskin, came with red laces, and had a silver Swoosh above the N.E.R.D. logo on the outer heel and on the tongue. The number itself was located on a tag underneath the tongue of the right foot.

N.E.R.D. × Nike Dunk High
Release date: 2004
Retail price: $110
Resale price: $2,700–$8,640 (€2,500–€8,000) as of 2023

Pharrell × Bape Road STA
• Release date: 2006
• Retail price: $212
• Resale price: $1,728 (€1,600) for new pairs

Pharrell × Bape Road STA

A pack of three shiny, colorful pairs, which are pretty rare and hard to find, especially in DS version (deadstock, meaning unused). They have the particular feature of having Pharrell Williams's head embroidered in Bape style on the heel. The pack was rereleased in 2022, with slightly different colors and without Pharrell Williams's head.

N.E.R.D. × Bape STA FS-001 Low "Red"

Bape collectors will tell you that this pair is a holy grail; that's how rare it is. It was made in patent leather in several different shades of red, in reference to the Pharrell red Bape camo—the "Pharrell Camo," which you could see at the time in the music video for Snoop Dogg and Pharrell's *Let's Get Blown*. And of course, the N.E.R.D. logo is embroidered on the heel.

N.E.R.D. × Bape STA FS-001 Low "Red"
Release date: 2006
Retail price: Unknown
Resale price: Too rare and too random

BBC × Timberland Six-Inch Boots "Bee Line"

Even though these boots benefited from a great ad campaign featuring artists such as Missy Elliott, Rihanna, and Beyoncé, not to mention Pharrell Williams himself, these shoes did not create much of a stir. Nevertheless, I find this "Bee Line" concept absolutely well executed, especially because the pair is made from organic materials, using plastic recovered from the ocean and recycled. A few pairs of "Bee Lines" are still released every now and then.

BBC × Timberland Six-Inch Boots "Bee Line"
Release date: 05/22/2015
Retail price: $240

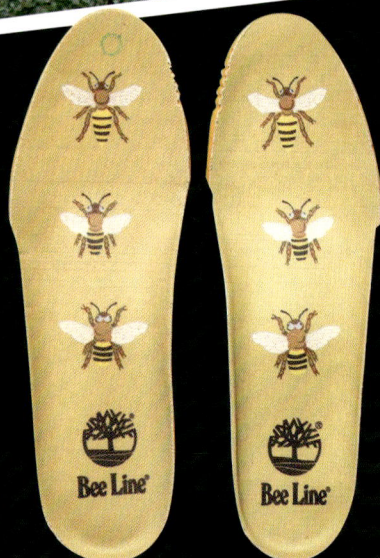

PHARRELL WILLIAMS × ADIDAS NMD HU

The most popular Pharrell Williams collaborations are still the ones with Adidas. There have been so many, and others are still being regularly released. However, some of them have been particularly successful.

Pharrell Williams × Adidas NMD HU "Race Yellow"

There has always been a great love story between Pharrell Williams and Adidas. In 2016, it was Pharrell's turn to propose a pair in his image, which he did with the Human Race. This model was the first version in yellow, which was released as a limited edition. The different pairs launched in collaboration with Pharrell since 2016 are all under the name HU, which stands for Health Ultimatum. They also feature a pattern that represents the acupuncture points of the arch of the foot on the insole.

True to himself, Pharrell proposed a positive, engaging message: love, sharing, unity, tolerance, humanity . . . these are the kinds of words you'll find throughout his line with Adidas.

Pharrell Williams × Adidas NMD HU "Race Yellow"

Release date: 07/22/2016
Retail price: $240
Resale price: $650–$1,400 (€600–€1,300) as of 2023

Pharrell Williams × Adidas NMD HU Pack

This pack contained five colorways, in keeping with the Human Race Yellow. Each upper contains embroidered words: "HU Race" on the scarlet, "HU HU" inside a triangle on the green, "HU MAN" on the tangerine, "Human Being" on the blue, and, lastly, "Human Species" on the black.

The black and scarlet shades were each released as a limited edition, and the green, blue, and tangerine in extremely limited quantities.

Pharrell Williams × Adidas NMD HU Pack

Release date: 09/29/2016
Retail price: $240
Resale price: $325–$1,400 (€300–€1,300) (unit) according to the pairs available as of 2023

Pharrell Williams × Adidas NMD HU "Y.O.U.N.E.R.D."

This pair, an exclusive release that came out during ComplexCon 2017 in Los Angeles, refers to the alternative hip-hop group N.E.R.D. (No One Ever Really Dies), which Pharrell fronts with Shay Haley and Chad Hugo. It's a triple black pair with a trail outsole, a Boost midsole topped off with a black Primeknit upper, and the inscriptions "Y.O.U.N.E.R.D." You can find the group's logo on the heel.

Pharrell Williams × Adidas NMD HU "Y.O.U.N.E.R.D."
Release date: 11/04/2017
Retail price: $240
Resale price: $540–$1,950 (€500–€1,800) as of 2023

Chanel × PW × Adidas NMD HU
Release date: 11/21/2017
Retail price: €1,000
Resale price: $3,800–$8,650 (€3,500–€8,000) as of 2023

Chanel × PW × Adidas NMD HU

Here's a veritable event in the world of sneakers: a triple collaboration among Pharrell Williams, Adidas, and the Chanel couture house. It was not Chanel's first collaboration with a sportswear brand: In 1997, Karl Lagerfeld proposed a collaboration between Chanel and Reebok for the "Insta Pump Fury" model. The NMD Pharrell × Chanel model was sold exclusively at Colette on November 25, 2017 (just before the famous Paris boutique closed on December 20, 2017). Just five hundred pairs were manufactured and sold worldwide. While the price was incredibly high, the funds collected went to charity.

PW × Adidas NMD HU China "Gold" F&F released in the "Happy" Pack

This magnificent pair is part of a pack of four colorways sold exclusively in China. This gold version is a F&F model that was limited to three hundred pairs.

PW × Adidas NMD HU China "Gold" F&F released in the "Happy" Pack
Release date: 05/12/2018
Retail price: pair not sold
Resale price: $1,080–$3,800 (€1,000–€3,500) as of 2020

A BATHING APE AND RAPPERS

As you may have already noticed, the Japanese brand created by Nigo Bape never rests where collaborations with rappers are concerned. For further proof, here are two pairs I really like.

Gunna × Bape STA Low

Gunna, the Atlanta rapper from the group YSL also did his collaboration with Bape. The result is truly beautiful: snakeskin-textured black leather under Bapo camo waffle patent leather in a beautiful mint green. "SLATT" ("Slime Love All the Time"), something of a motto for YSL, is inscribed on the heels, and Gunna's name appears co-branded with Bape on the tongue.

Gunna × Bape STA Low
Release date: 02/06/2021 Retail price: $289 Resale price: $378–$918 (€350–€850) as of 2023

Curren$y × Bape STA Low

New Orleans rapper Curren$y is a big fan of the brand, which fits his style and, simultaneously, chill and bold flow. He showcases his label Jet Life in this simple and well-executed Bape STA collaboration. The Jet Life logo appears on the heel and tongue. It's a really nice pair of STAs! For your information, "STA" refers to the star you'll find on each pair. Note too that this pair is not in patent leather—rare enough for Bape that it's worth pointing out.

Curen$y × Bape STA Low
Release date: 07/11/2020 Retail price: $255 Resale price: $270–$540 (€250–€500) as of 2023

KANYE WEST: COLLABORATIONS AND CONTROVERSIES

I have already written extensively about the controversial character Kanye West in my previous books, so I'll simply retrace the path of the Chicago rapper's best collaborations here. As for Adidas, note that prices have plummeted at the time I am writing this (May 2023), given the controversy and the termination of the three-stripe brand's contract with the artist.

Nike Air Max 180 "College Dropout" F&F

Nike supposedly created this pair of Nike Air Max 180s to celebrate the success of the album The College Dropout, released one year prior. It also contains Dropout Bear, Kanye's mascot, on the tongue. The story behind this shoe gets pretty hazy. An unknown number of pairs were supposedly produced solely for Kanye West, in his size only (US 12).

Nike Air Max 180 "College Dropout" F&F
Release date: 2005
Retail price: pair not sold
Resale price: unable to be found

Kanye West × A Bathing Ape Bapesta "Dropout Bear"

Here's the first official Kanye collaboration, also designed in tribute to The College Dropout album. Released as a limited edition, it is one of the most sought-after pairs nowadays. There was a second release when his friends Virgil Abloh and Don Crawley opened their shop, RSVP Gallery, in 2009.

Kanye West × A Bathing Ape Bapesta "Dropout Bear"
Release date: December 2006
Retail price: unknown
Resale price: $4,320–$13,000 (€4,000–€12,000) as of 2023

Kanye West × Reebok S. Carter Classic Low "Dropout Bear" Samples

During the same period when Jay-Z was collaborating with Reebok and had his signature shoe with them (the "Shawn Corey Carter"), Kanye West was tapped to design four pairs in collaboration with Reebok and Jay-Z. You can really get a sense from his choice of colors and patent leather of how he was inspired at that time by Bape. The boxes say "Custom made for: Kanye West," along with the references, colorways, and the size—US 12. These pairs are samples made for Kanye West that were not sold, seeing how he was already in contract on a collaboration with Nike at the time.

Kanye West × Reebok S. Carter Classic Low "Dropout Bear" Samples
Release date: 2008 Retail price: pairs not sold Resale price: unable to be found

Nike Air Yeezy 1 "Grammy" Sample

In 2007, Kanye signed a contract for a collaboration with American giant Nike. He did a few samples from 2007 to 2008, collaborating closely with Tinker Hatfield. They notably worked on samples of the Jordan VIs as well as the Air Huarache 08s, for example. Yet, the first pair that was actually unveiled to the general public was the Nike Air Yeezy 1. The shoe was coined the "Grammy," quite simply because he wore them to the 50th Grammy Awards in 2008, so that the pair would get a lot of visibility and immediately generate a buzz. These sale strategies have since become very popular, and they are extremely effective. The Nike Air Yeezy 1 was later sold in other colorways.

Nike Air Yeezy 1

The Nike Air Yeezy 1s were very popular, even though, in 2009, a lot fewer people were interested in sneakers. This was a limited edition sold in shops that had a "Tier 0" account. In Paris, around a hundred pairs in each color were distributed among three stores: Opium, Colette, and Nike Stadium. These pairs marked the arrival of the first time that people truly "camped out" in France, sleeping in front of a store to be sure to get a pair (a phenomenon that had already occurred in 2005 for the Nike Air Max 1 Amsterdams).

The aesthetic details of this pair are very interesting. You can see how the upper rests on top of a glow-in-the-dark Air Jordan II outsole, while the Velcro band in textured leather lends some character to the pair. The shoes also features Y-shaped lace locks above the shoelaces.

The Nike Air Yeezy 1s were released in three colorways: Net Tan, Zen Gray, and Blink. The black Blink was the most popular colorway, because the black, the bright pink (the company called it Solar Red), and the "glow-in-the-dark" paired perfectly. Sneakers with these colors are often nicknamed "Yeezys" nowadays, even when the shoe is not a Kanye West collaboration.

Nike Air Yeezy 1
Release date: 04/04/2009 Retail price: $250 Resale price: $2,200–$5,400 (€2,000–€5,000) according to the colorways available as of 2023

Nike Air Yeezy 1 "Grammy" Sample
Release date: 02/10/2008 Retail price: pair not sold Resale price: sold at auction for $1,800,000

Kanye West × Louis Vuitton "Don"

That same year, Kanye West teamed up with Louis Vuitton and released a collection of high-end sneakers. There is no denying that Kanye West has played an important role in bridging streetwear and luxury brands. The three models he designed with Louis Vuitton bear the name of three people on his team at the time. In this case, "Don" pays tribute to Don Crawley, his former manager and currently designer of the brand Just Don, to whom we also owe several excellent collaborations with Nike and Jordan Brand. Virgil Abloh was also part of this team. I've counted five colorways for the "Don": Cream, Red, Anthracite, Patchwork Brown, and Triple Black. These are very coveted pairs nowadays.

Kanye West × Louis Vuitton "Don"

Release date: 07/01/2009
Retail price: $870–$960 for "Patchwork Brown."
Resale price: $2,200–$8,600 (€2,000–€8,000), depending on colorway, as of 2023, although it's not rare to see prices posted in the range of $18,400–$21,600 (€17,000–€20,000)

Kanye West × Louis Vuitton "Jasper"

Release date: 07/01/2009
Retail price: $990–$1,140 for Patchwork Gray
Resale price: $4,320–$10,800 (€4,000–€10,000), depending on colorway, as of 2023

Kanye West × Louis Vuitton "Jasper"

The "Jasper" model, in tribute to Kanye West's friend and hairstylist, came out in three colorways: Black, Cream, and Patchwork Gray. The Patchwork Gray with the fluorescent pink outsole is a bit more expensive, both because that material is more costly and it has a larger amount of Velcro at the top.

Kanye West × Louis Vuitton "Mr. Hudson"

This is an homage from Kanye West to his friend Mr. Hudson, a British singer on the same label as Kanye, Good Music. The white version was released as a limited edition of seventy-five pairs, while the gray and pink version was limited to twenty-four F&F pairs.

Kanye West × Louis Vuitton "Mr. Hudson"
- Release date: 07/01/2009
- Retail price: $840
- Resale price: price listed as $16,200–$27,000 (€15,000–€25,000), but hard to find

Nike Air Yeezy 2 "Pure Platinum"

In 2012, Kanye returned to Nike and made a strong impact with the Nike Air Yeezy 2 in Pure Platinum and Solar Red. There was major demand for this very limited-edition product. It was a huge success, and they are highly coveted—as are all Nike Air Yeezys.

Nike Air Yeezy 2 "Pure Platinum"
Release date: 06/09/2012
Retail price: $250
Resale price: $3,200–$6,500 (€3,000–€6,000) as of 2023

Nike Air Yeezy 2 "Solar Red"
Release date: 06/09/2012
Retail price: $250
Resale date: $3,800–$8,600 (€3,500–€8,000) as of 2023

Nike Air Yeezy 2 "Red October"

The Nike Air Yeezy 2 "Red October" is one of the Yeezys that packs the biggest punch, due to its color. Personally, it's one of my favorite pairs.

Thanks to the success of the Nike Air Yeezy 1s, demand grew increasingly strong. There were a lot of leaks on social media, and a true frenzy took hold. Then one Sunday, as a surprise, Nike released this pair as if it were nothing. As an aside, that was the day I got my chance to connect to the Nike website at just the right moment. I was so surprised to see the pair; I thought it might be a future product. This resulted in me taking too long, and my hesitation cost me. I lost the shoes even though I'd had time to put them in my cart. To conclude, I'll note an interesting feature of the pair—you can see that the sole was borrowed from Agassi's Air Tech Challenge 2.

Air Tech Challenge 2 DG "Hot Lava"

Nike Air Yeezy 2 "Red October"
Release date: 02/09/2014
Retail price: $250
Resale price: $5,400–$21,600 (€5,000–€20,000) as of 2023

Adidas Yeezy Boost 750 "Light Brown"

The first! The first of them all! There were nearly two years between signing the contract and the first Yeezy release! Designing a shoe takes time. Furthermore, we were moving from a very Nike world to a very Kanye world. Incidentally, you'll find some overlap with the Nike Air Yeezys, such as the Velcro and even the overall shape. Although many people (and I'm one of them) took some time to get used to the Adidas Yeezys, the sneakers nevertheless sold out right after their release. Nine thousand pairs of this shoe were produced, and the model was never rereleased. Once again trying to whet fans' appetites and generate a buzz, the pair was first released as a preview at the New York All-Star Game on February 14, 2015, then worldwide on February 28, 2015. It's essentially a b-ball shoe.

The very high price tag also deterred many people, but it was proof that Kanye wanted to move upmarket. For this model, three limited-edition colorways were subsequently produced: first the Black, then the Light Gray Gum, and, lastly, the Chocolate in October 2016. Since that time, the model has fallen off the radar. Generally speaking, you can see preview pairs at Kanye West fashion shows, which was the case for this pair during the "Yeezy Season 1" show. Kanye in effect pairs up his sneakers with clothing from his "streetwear luxe" brand, Yeezy Supply, which works really well. His various collections express a state of mind and a philosophy. The "Yeezy Season 1" was designed in collaboration with Demna Gvasalia, founder of the brand Vetements and current creative director at Balenciaga.

Adidas Yeezy Boost 750 "Light Brown"
Release date: 02/14/2015
Retail price: $350
Resale price: $1,200–$2,400 (€1,100–€2,200) as of 2023 (the most expensive of the Adidas Yeezys)

Adidas Yeezy Boost 350 "Turtle Dove"

As with the 750s, Nike Yeezy afficionados truly had a hard time adapting—and some of them still have not. These pairs undoubtedly mark an evolution and change of course on the part of Kanye. At the time, no one knew how many pairs had been produced in the limited edition, which roused a certain degree of skepticism. This confusion made it easy to get hold of a pair the day they came out. It turns out now that the "Turtle Dove" was very coveted.

For this model, three limited-edition colorways were produced: First there was the legendary Pirate Black, followed by the Moonrock, and, lastly, in December 2015, the Oxford Tan. There was also a flash restock of the Pirate Black V1 on June 19, 2016. The name "Turtle Dove" refers to the neck of turtledove birds, which often have a gray and black patterned splotch, like the one you can see on the Primeknit of this pair.

The Adidas Yeezy Boost 350 "Turtle Dove" was rereleased in 2022.

Adidas Yeezy Boost 350 "Turtle Dove"
Release date: 06/27/2015
Retail price: $230
Resale price: $540–$1,600 (€500–€1,500) as of 2023

Adidas Yeezy Boost 350 V2 "Beluga"

There it is, the V2 of the 350, the most popular pair in the world nowadays. Initially, the drop was rather limited and very hard to find. These days, we talk in terms of several hundred thousands pairs per drop—and, despite that, most releases sell out nearly immediately. As of 2019–20, pure collectors were starting to shun this version, which has become too popular and comes out in a new color nearly every month. The pair has in fact become part of a mass phenomenon, although, happily, limited-edition versions appear from time to time, such as the "Reflectives" in particular. As far as colorways go, the ones collectors most seek out for the first V2s are the Black/Red, which was released in November 2016; the Oreo, sold in December 2016; and the Pirate Black V2, which came out in February 2017. In my opinion, one of the nicest models is the "Zebra," even though it was the victim of some controversial restocks.

Adidas Yeezy Boost 350 V2 "Beluga"
Release date: 09/24/2016
Retail price: $220
Resale price: $325–$760 (€300–€700) as of 2023

Adidas Yeezy Powerphase Calabasas "White"

The Powerphase has been a classic Adidas model since the 1980s, just like the Continental 80, which was designed to gain market share over Reebok in the fitness world. Kanye perhaps wanted to give a more classic feel to his collection.

You'll find the name "Calabasas" on the shoe, which is the Los Angeles neighborhood where Kanye lived and where his ex-wife, Kim Kardashian, grew up.

Adidas Yeezy Powerphase Calabasas "White"
Release date: 03/28/2017
Retail price: $120

Adidas Yeezy Boost 700 "Wave Runner"
Release date: 11/01/2017
Retail price: $300
Resale price: $380–$490 (€350–€450) as of 2023

Adidas Yeezy Boost 700 "Wave Runner"

Released in the midst of the resurgence of the "dad shoe" and "chunky kicks," this model really took off. Nowadays, our eyes are more used to this kind of silhouette. Despite a few restocks, the 700 "Wave Runner" remains much in demand, because it's very well executed visually and aesthetically. It maintains a consistent market value, as is the case for the 350 V2 "Zebra."

Adidas Yeezy 700 V2 "Slate"

Release date: 12/29/2018
Retail price: $300
Resale price: approximately $325 (€300) as of 2023

Adidas Yeezy 500 "Blush"

Release date: 02/16/2018
Retail price: $200

Adidas Yeezy Boost 380 "Alien"

This pair marks a new era for the Yeezy, which needed a bit of a refresh. Originally, it was supposed to be called the "350 V3," but since it's fairly different it was rechristened the "380." The "Alien" was released in a very limited quantity. In France, for example, SNS Paris was the only store to sell the shoes.

Adidas Yeezy Boost 380 "Alien"

Release date: 12/12/2019
Retail price: $230
Resale price: $270–$325 (€250–€300) as of 2023

Adidas Yeezy 500 High "Slate"

Release date: 12/16/2019
Retail price: $220
Here is a high-top version of the Yeezy 500.

Adidas Yeezy 700 V3 "Azael"

Here's a true breath of fresh air for Yeezys and a real personal favorite. These shoes are completely different, with a clear patterned plastic top held in by an exoskeleton coated with glow-in-the-dark paint, which turns fluorescent green at night. It was released as a very limited edition, via raffle in just three Paris shops and simultaneously on the Adidas app. Note that it does not contain a Boost in the sole, which allowed the price to be decreased from €300 to €200.

Adidas Yeezy 700 V3 "Azael"
Release date: 12/23/2019
Retail price: $200
Resale price: $270–$430 (€250–€400) as of 2023

Adidas Yeezy Boost 700 MNVN "Triple Black"

This variant of the 700 came out in 2020. Discovered in 2018 on the Instagram account of 6ix9ine, this shoe is the result of a collaboration between Steven Smith and Christian Tresser. The entirely thermally glued nylon upper features 700 branding in 3M.

The name MNVN means "Mini-Van" and comes from a private joke between the pair's designers.

Adidas Yeezy Boost 700 MNVN "Triple Black"
Release date: 02/08/2020
Retail price: $220

Adidas Yeezy Quantum "Lifestyle"

This baby of the family exists in two versions: B-Ball and Lifestyle, which is pictured here. Although there are very few differences between the two models in terms of how they look, the former is simply stronger on the court. Both pairs were released exclusively during the Chicago NBA All-Star Game. These Lifestyle and B-Ball models were part of the most limited Yeezy editions, with quantities approaching five thousand pairs in total, sold only in Chicago. As an aside, the first version of the B-Ball caused a problem with the NBA, because 3M, which is a reflective material, refracted photographers' flash too much and concealed the players' sneakers. The following models were adapted to contain less 3M, along with other modifications.

Adidas Yeezy Quantum "Lifestyle"
Release date: 02/16/2020
Retail price: $250
Resale price: $650–$870 (€600–€800) as of 2023

BIG SEAN

Big Sean × Adidas Pro Model II "Detroit Player"

There have been several collaborations between Big Sean, the Detroit rapper, and Adidas, but this is the first and most important—and above all, the most successful, in my opinion. The red and gold shoe is made from premium Italian snakeskin-textured leather with pyramid-shaped deubrés marked with the letters OE and the words "I say I'm still dreaming bigger than I'm living" inscribed in the lining. This exceptional pair of Adidas comes in a special box and has plenty of details. The model was limited to 380 pairs and named the Pro Model Big Sean "Detroit Player" because the rapper grew up in Detroit. He certainly did not go wrong on this shoe, which was released after Kanye's LVs but before the Yeezy Red Octobers.

Big Sean × Adidas Pro Model II "Detroit Player"
Release date: 12/01/2012
Retail price: $160
Resale price: $650–$2,200 (€600–€2,000) as of 2023, but very hard to find

NIKE'S
TOP COLLABS

Booba × Nike Air Force 1 Low PRM "1 World"

Let's start with a collaboration between a French rapper and the Oregon brand Nike. If there's one thing that I realized as I wrote this part of the book, it's that Nike really works with a lot of rappers. They are the faces of the brand and participate in promos or the launch of new models, which the press in effect refers to as collaborations. But having your own collaboration pair does not mean just taking photos or doing videos for the brand. And I think that just one French rapper can boast having actually collaborated with Nike: Booba.

Booba was offered this amazing opportunity for the "1 World" project run by Nike. The "1 World" project has artists from several countries express themselves by designing a pair of sneakers. For the 2008 event, there were eighteen artists in all, two of whom represented France—Booba and Busy P, who has also done his own Air Force 1s. Considering that KAWS's and Michael Lau's Nike Air Force 1 Low "1 World" sneakers come from the same program, this is no small achievement!

Booba called on the tattoo artist Laura Santana to work on his pair, which contains a "09" embroidered on the tongue, in reference to the name of his album from that period; the Senegalese flag with the "K" from his brand at that time, Unkut; Laura Santana's tattoo art; and references to the artist in various places on a very nice premium red leather. This limited collaboration of 176 was a success, and several American fans of AF1s are actively searching for them.

Booba × Nike Air Force 1 Low PRM "1 World"
Release date: 12/06/2008
Retail price: €200
Resale price: $1,600–$2,500 (€1,500–€2,300) as of 2023

THE CREATIVE WORLD OF SKEPTA

The patron saint of London grime has done some great collaborations with Nike, with which he signed a deal in 2016–17, still in the spirit of the city and the UK "Top Boy" style.

Skepta × Nike Air Max Ultra 97

Release date: 09/02/2017
Retail price: $180
Resale price: $270–$380 (€250-€350) as of 2023

Skepta × Nike Air Max 97/BW

Release date: 05/18/2018
Retail price: $190
Resale price: $325–$700 (€300–€650) as of 2023

Skepta × Nike Air Max Deluxe

Release date: 09/08/2018
Retail price: $190
Resale price: $160–$325 (€150–€300) as of 2023

Skepta × Nike Show TL

Release date: 09/05/2019
Retail price: $200
Resale price: $325–$540 (€300–€500) as of 2023

Skepta × Nike Air Max Tailwind 5

Release date: 04/02/2021
Retail price: $180
Resale price: $325–$540 (€300–€500) as of 2023

Skepta × Nike Air Max Tailwind 5 "Bloody Chrome Pack"

Release date: 06/12/2021
Retail price: $180
Resale price: $216–$650 (€200–€600) as of 2023

Nike SK Phantom GT Elite FG "Bloody Chrome Pack"

Retail price: $270
Resale price: $216–$380 (€200–€350) as of 2023

TRAVIS SCOTT AND NIKE, BANKABLE COLLABORATIONS

Superstar Travis Scott's sneaker game went through the roof with his Nike and Jordan Brand collaboration—to say the least. Almost all "Travis Scott × Nike" releases unleashed a kind of competitive spirit among sneaker addicts, even though in 2023 some began to turn their backs on the collaboration, given the overexploitation of its success. In 2020, *Forbes* magazine estimated that the collaboration between Travis Scott and Nike brought in more than $10 million per year for the artist. Here's a small refresher on all the Travis × Nike releases.

Travis Scott × Nike Air Force 1 Low AF100

Release date: 12/02/2017
Retail price: $150
Resale price: $1,500–$2,300 (€1,400-€2,100) as of 2023

Travis Scott × Air Jordan IV Retro "Cactus Jack"

Release date: 06/09/2018
Retail price: $225
Resale price: $860–$1,400 (€800–€1,300) as of 2023

Travis Scott × Nike Air Force 1 Low Sail

Release date: 08/10/2018
Retail price: $150
Resale price: $750–$1,800 (€700–€1,700) as of 2023

Travis Scott × Air Jordan XXXIII Olive

Release date: 02/14/2019
Retail price: $185
Resale price: $195–$325 (€180–€300) as of 2023

Travis Scott × Air Jordan 1 Retro High SP Dark Mocha

Release date: 05/11/2019
Retail price: $175
Resale price: $1,300–$2,600 (€1,200–€2,400) as of 2023

Travis Scott × Air Jordan 1 Retro Low SP Dark Mocha

Release date: 07/20/2019
Retail price: $130
Resale price: $1,620–$2,050 (€1,500–€1,900) as of 2023

Travis Scott × Nike SB Dunk Low (Regular Box)

Release date: 02/29/2020
Retail price: $150
Resale price: $1,400–$1,950 (€1,300–€1,800) as of 2023

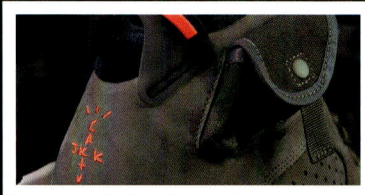

Travis Scott × Air Jordan VI Retro Olive

Release date: 10/11/2019
Retail price: $250
Resale price: $430–$650 (€400–€600) as of 2023

Travis Scott × Nike Air Max 270 React ENG "Cactus Trail"

Release date: 05/29/2020
Retail price: $170
Resale price: $325–$490 (€300–€450) as of 2023

Travis Scott × Nike Air Force 1 "Cactus Jack"

Release date: 11/16/2019
Retail price: $160
Resale price: $430–$650 (€400–€600) as of 2023

Travis Scott × Air Jordan VI Retro British Khaki

Release date: 04/30/2021
Retail price: $250
Resale price: $325–$490 (€300–€450) as of 2023

Fragment Design × Travis Scott x Air Jordan 1 Retro High SP

Release date: 07/29/2021
Retail price: $200
Resale price: $1,950–$2,700 (€1,800–2,500) as of 2023

Travis Scott × Nike Air Max 1 "Cactus Jack" Baroque Brown

Release date: 05/27/2022
Retail price: $160
Resale price: $325–$540 (€300–€500) as of 2023

Fragment Design × Travis Scott x Air Jordan 1 Retro Low SP

Release date: 08/13/2021
Retail price: $150
Resale price: $1,200–$2,050 (€1,100–€1,900)

Travis Scott × Nike Air Trainer 1 SP "Wheat"

Release date: 05/27/2022
Retail price: $160
Resale price: $108–$170 (€100–€160) as of 2023

Travis Scott × Nike Air Max 1 "Cactus Jack" Wheat Lemon Drop

Release date: 05/23/2022
Retail price: $160
Resale price: $325–$430 (€300–€400) as of 2023

Travis Scott × Nike Air Trainer 1 SP "Gray Haze"

• Release date: 05/27/2022
• Retail price: $160
• Resale price: $108–$170 (€100–€160) as of 2023

Travis Scott × Nike Air Max 1 "Cactus Jack" Saturn Gold

Release date: 05/27/2022
Retail price: $160
Resale price: $205–$380 (€190–€350) as of 2023

Travis Scott × Air Jordan 1 Retro Low SP Olive

Release date: 04/26/2023
Retail price: $150
Resale price: $490–$1,080 (€450–€1,000) as of 2023

Travis Scott × Air Jordan 1 Retro Low SP Black Phantom

Release date: 12/15/2022
Retail price: $150
Resale price: $500–$650 (€460–€600) as of 2023

AT THE TIME THAT I'M WRITING THIS, IN MAY 2023, IT'S BEEN ANNOUNCED THAT A NEW SILHOUETTE IS BEING RELEASED FROM THE ARCHIVES IN COLLABORATION WITH TRAVIS SCOTT: THE NIKE MAC ATTACK.

TRAVIS SCOTT "FRIENDS & FAMILY" (F&F) AND OTHER GRAILS

PlayStation × Travis Scott × Nike Dunk Low

Twenty-four "Flame" pairs were reserved for the superstar's entourage, plus another five pairs that could be won in the United States from the artist's merch website. For the release of the PS5, Travis Scott debuted a capsule collection done in collaboration with Sony PlayStation.

Travis Scott × Air Jordan 1 Retro Low SP Reverse Mocha

Release date: 07/21/2022
Retail price: $150
Resale price: $920–$1,200 (€850–€1,100) as of 2023

Travis Scott × Air Jordan IV Retro Purple F&F

Release date: 2018
Retail price: pair not sold
Resale price: approximately $21,600 (€20,000) as of 2023

Travis Scott × Air Jordan IV Retro Olive F&F

Release date: 2018
Retail price: pair not sold
Resale price: approximately $27,000 (€25,000) as of 2023

Travis Scott × Air Jordan IV Retro "Cactus Jack" F&F

Release date: 2018
Retail price: pair not sold
Resale price: $3,800–$10,800 (€3,500–€10,000) as of 2023

Travis Scott × Air Jordan VI Retro Yellow F&F

Release date: 2020
Retail price: pair not sold
Resale price: no pairs available for sale
You may have already seen this pair on the feet of rapper Offset.

Fragment Design × Travis Scott x Air Jordan 1 Low (Sample)

This pair, never before seen, showed up on the feet of Fragment Design creator Hiroshi Fujiwara, who wore them during the NBA Japan Games in September 2022. Only time will tell whether it's a future release or a permanent sample.

Playstation × Travis Scott × Nike Dunk Low

Release date: 11/13/2020
Retail price: F&F
Resale price: $5,400–$10,800 (€5,000–€10,000) as of June 2023

Fragment Design × Travis Scott × Air Jordan 1 Low (Sample)

Release date: no release; it's a sample
Retail price: pair not sold
Resale price: no pairs available for sale

MACKLEMORE'S AIR JORDAN VI

Macklemore × Air Jordan VI Retro "Cactus" F&F

Only eleven pairs of this shoe were produced, for rapper Macklemore and his entourage. This sneaker is magnificent, with details "to kill" on the heel—a shark, in tribute to the artist's team, the Shark Face Gang.

Macklemore × Air Jordan VI Retro "Cactus" F&F

Release date: 2014
Retail price: pair not sold
Resale price: unable to be found; prices at the discretion of the buyer and seller

Macklemore × Air Jordan VI Retro "Clay" F&F

The rapper wore this pair to the 2014 Jordan Brand Classic. Only thirty-five pairs of the sneaker were produced, along with a total of forty-six F&F pairs of the "Cactus" and "Clay" models.

Macklemore × Air Jordan VI Retro "Clay" F&F

Release date: 2014
Retail price: pair not sold
Resale price: unable to be found; price at the discretion of the buyer and seller

THE LEGENDARY PROTOTYPE OF THE WU-TANG CLAN

Nike Dunk High "Wu-Tang Clan" (Sample)

This is one of the most legendary pairs you can find in France. Uncle Texaco, DJ, street marketing expert, and collector, is here to talk with us about this grail shoe.

Tex: At the time I was still working for Loud Records, Wu-Tang Clan's label, created by Steve Rifkind, for the region of France. Know that Steve Rifkind's marketing firm, SRC (Steve Rifkind Company), was a consultant for Nike when the brand was starting to make retro models. Nike got together the label's staff, the street teams, and basically asked us what models he should release, in which colors, etc. They showed us lots of prototypes and asked for our opinion. And it so happens that was when Nike was going to release the first Dunk College Colors in a retro version. This was 1997. The representatives from Loud Records saw the Dunk High Goldenrod in yellow and black, which were Wu-Tang Clan's colors. Their second studio album, *Wu-Tang Forever*, had just come out. They quite simply asked Nike to make them a Wu-Tang Clan pair for the album. It was not a collaboration in the strict sense of the word, but promotional F&F pairs were distributed almost one and a half years after the release of *Wu-Tang Forever*. The story goes that only thirty-six pairs were produced, but, in my opinion, there were more of them. They were distributed to the members of the Wu-Tang Clan, people from the label, and a few American bigwigs—like Funkmaster Flex, for example.

Loud Records offered me the prototype that was used for the promotion. On a sidenote, prototypes don't normally have a box. However, since the pair was used for the promotion and had to be lugged around everywhere, Nike did a twist on an ACG (All Conditions Gear) box, gluing a label onto the outer cardboard part, even though there was an ACG logo inside.

Nike Dunk High "Wu-Tang Clan" (Sample)

Release date: 1999
Prototype: promo in June 1998
Retail price: pair not sold (F&F)
Resale price: Too rare to get a proper estimate. The price varies depending on the condition of the pair and how much a buyer wants that model. There's also just one prototype of this one, which significantly increases its value. Tex regularly receives offers ranging from $10,800 to $37,800 (€10,000–€35,000) for the most recent ones. But you never know: If a millionaire is determined to get a pair, the price could get very high! It's surely one of the biggest pairs you can find on French territory, in my opinion.

DRAKE, FROM OVO TO NOCTA

The superstar Drake, alias Champagne Papi, is one of the biggest names at Nike and Jordan Brand—so much so that he now has his own brand at Nike, Nocta, just like Jordan Brand. Drake's collaborations with Jordan Brand began with samples, F&Fs, etc. for music videos and tours. The first one, in 2014, was a PE (Player Exclusive: a single pair, normally reserved for an athlete) of an Air Jordan III Anaconda designed by Mark Smith (the creative director behind some really nice pairs) for a music video for the Nicki Minaj track "Anaconda." It was just a quick cameo, but it certainly did not go unnoticed. Then (still in 2014 and still for the Jordan III), a pack of two Air Jordan III pairs came out, known as the "Drake VS Lil Wayne" on the occasion of the two artists' joint summer tour of the same name. Later that year, there was another PE for an Air Jordan Retro III, the Air Jordan III "OVO Gold," which was released for the OVO Fest. It goes without saying that the Jordan III × Drake 2014s are exceptional shoes.

Drake is also the founder of the OVO brand (October's Very Own), and he signed on to his first official Jordan Brand collaboration with that label, in September 2015. At the time, sneaker addicts were particularly drawn to the OVO × Jordan collaboration, especially since it was the height of the sneaker craze.

Jordan XI Snakeskin

Air Jordan XI "OVO Gold"

Jordan IV Splatter

Jordan VIII "Calipari" White PE

Jordan VIII "Calipari" Black PE

OVO × Air Jordan × Retro "White"

Drake's star continues to rise. Add to that the cool sensibility of the OVO brand and a limited edition here and there, and it's a recipe for success. That's how it starts.

Here's the result of a collaboration with OVO, the Canadian superstar's brand. Just like the "Black" model below, these sneakers have a lot of pretty stylish details, including a translucent glitter outsole showing the OVO logo. You'll also love the patches made of faux shagreen, a shark- or stingray-type fish skin, which lends a rough, cartilage-like texture. But it's above all the shimmery reflection of the shagreen that makes this collaboration so stylish.

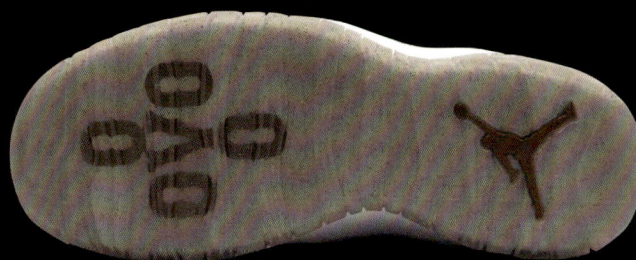

> **OVO × Air Jordan × Retro "White"**
> Release date: 09/12/2015
> Retail price: $225
> Resale price: $432–$540 (€400–€500) as of 2023

OVO × Air Jordan × Retro "Black"

This shoe came out during the NBA All-Star Games, which is no coincidence, because the 2016 ASGs were held in Toronto, Drake's hometown. The details make all the difference in these models—here the textured leather has the look of shagreen, the rough skin of a stingray or shark, which lends a high-class feel to these pairs.

> **OVO × Air Jordan × Retro "Black"**
> Release date: 02/13/2016
> Retail Price: $225
> Resale Price: $325–$490 (€300–€450) as of 2023

OVO × Air Jordan XII Retro "Black"

This pair had the same launch plan as for the Jordan Xs; the black was scheduled to be released in time for the All-Star Game.

> **OVO × Air Jordan XII Retro "Black"**
> Release date: 02/18/2017
> Retail price: $225
> Resale Price: $432–$700 (€400–€650) as of June 2023

OVO × Air Jordan XII Retro "White"

This is certainly my favorite pair of all the Drake collaborations, and it was the highest-valued OVO collaboration in 2023.

As was the case for its older siblings, the AJ10 OVOs, the Air Jordan XII OVO "White" sneakers were created in collaboration with the superstar, under the control of his label and his OVO clothing brand. Released as a limited edition, this model was also made in a black version three months later. They're a really nice pair, stamped "OVO" in white and gold, with that famous shagreen-style textured leather, which adds a lot of character to the overall shoe.

OVO × Air Jordan XII Retro "White"

Release date: 10/01/2016
Retail price: $225
Resale price: $750–$1,500 (€700–€1,400) as of 2023

OVO × Air Jordan VIII Retro "White"

Both of the Jordan VIII OVOs were released for the All-Star Game.

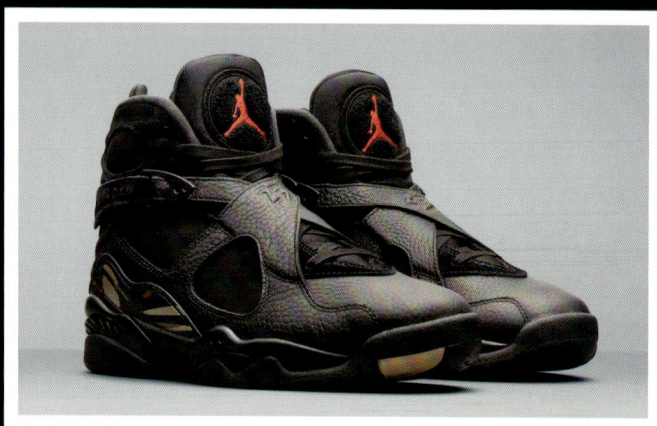

OVO × Air Jordan VIII Retro "Black"

Release date: 02/16/2018
Retail price: $225
Resale Price: $325–$490 (€300–€450) as of June 2023

OVO × Air Jordan VIII Retro "White"

Release date: 02/16/2018
Retail price: $225
Resale price: $325–$650 (€300–€600) as of June 2023

OVO × Air Jordan XIV Retro "God's Plan" PE

This pair was made for rapper Drake under the OVO label. Nobody knows exactly how many pairs are in circulation, but it's definitely fewer than ten. You can really feel the singer's taste in the Kentucky Wildcats blue.

This is an ultimate grail shoe, much like the Jordan IIIs I spoke about a bit earlier. There are other Drake PEs, such as the OVO × Air Jordan XVII Retro, which Sotheby's sold for $7,500; the Jordan IV Splatter, which Sotheby's also sold, for $32,500; or even the Jordan XI Snakeskins, which come in two different versions.

The Jordan VII "Calipari" White and Black PE, earmarked for coach John Calipari, sold for $13,860 (for the white) and $7,560 (for the black). The OVO × Air Jordan XI Gold went for $20,160, also at Sotheby's. After 2017, relations between Nike and Drake cooled a bit, to the point that Drake was seen wearing Adidas—perhaps a sign of provocation? Today, their relationship has improved, and Drake has established his own brand, Nocta, which he uses to offer previously unseen models. However, I do think that fans miss the OVO × Jordan Brand era!

OVO × Air Jordan XIX Retro "God's Plan" PE

Release date: 2018
Retail price: pair never sold
Resale price: $26,000 (€24,000) as of 2023

NIKE SB AND RAP

Three rap groups have done collaborations with Nike SB, well before the SB craziness of 2020, and these three pairs are now among those most sought after by collectors. Nike SB's very first collaboration with the group De La Soul was followed by one with MF Doom, then another with Madlib. All these artists were on the fringes of gangsta rap and had a style that fit the skater spirit really well.

De La Soul × Nike SB Dunk High & Low Pro (Pink Box 2004/2005)

Both of these are inspired by the neo-psychedelic illustrations from De La Soul's first album, *3 Feet High and Rising*. In 2015, Nike rereleased two pairs of De La Souls, but with the High and Low colorways reversed.

De La Soul × Nike SB Dunk High & Low Pro (Pink Box 2004/2005)

Release date: 11/2005
Retail price:
High-top model: $120
Low top model: $100
Resale:
High-top model: $750–$2,700 (€700–€2,500) as of June 2023
Low-top model: $490–$975 (€450–€900) as of June 2023

MF DOOM × Nike SB Dunk High Pro
(Black Box 2006/2007)

Metal Face DOOM, a London native who grew up in New York, always knew how to stay true to his vision—he was one of the timeless rappers. Unfortunately, he left us in 2020, which inevitably caused a rise in the resale price of this legendary pair, which the rapper designed personally with one of his friends—along with the Nike SB teams, of course. This pair is really cool, done in the image of the fanboy of superheroes—and, above all, supervillains. Speaking of which, the details on the SPR VLN pair go in this direction: the mask on the tongue, the imitation ostrich skin leather, red shoelaces, a special gum sole, and even the word "doom" embroidered on the side . . . truly a wonder!

MF Doom × Nike SB Dunk High Pro (Black Box 2006/2007)

Release date: 07/24/2007
Retail price: $150
Resale price: $1,600–$2,700 (€1,500–€2,500) as of June 2023

Madlib × Nike SB Dunk High Pro « Quasimoto » F&F (Black Box 2006/2007)

Release date: 07/24/2007
Retail price: $150
Resale price: $1,600–$2,700 (€1,500–€2,500) as of June 2023

Madlib × Nike SB Dunk High Pro "Quasimoto" F&F
(Black Box 2006/2007)

And to conclude, the ultimate grail item, released in celebration of the tenth anniversary of top West Coast label Stones Throw Records. Quasimoto is a project with rapper and musician Madlib, a prominent member of the label who collaborated on an entire album with MF Doom, *MadVillainy*, and his animated alter ego, Lord Quas. MF Doom was also an artist with Stones Throw Records. On a sidenote, these three pairs are connected, because Rob Sissi, a member of Nike SB's teams who had worked on the "De La Soul" pair, had first personally asked the group if it thought that MF Doom would be interested in the idea of doing a collaboration with Nike SB. For the Quasimoto, people say very different things about the quantities (some talk in terms of fifty pairs, others of just twenty-four); nevertheless, it is still a very rare pair that was distributed only to members of the West Coast label. You'd need to ask the label's founder, Peanut Butter Wolf, who must know the answer to that question. One pair was auctioned at Sotheby's for $15,120, and I saw a pair of size US 12s available at Stockx with an offer of €196,428. The embroidery on the heel represents the character Quasimoto.

DJ KHALED, COLLECTOR AND DESIGNER

DJ Khaled is an important sneaker fan and collector, primarily of Jordans. Since 2017 he's released several gems in collaboration with Jordan Brand. Needless to say, he began with his favorite model: the Air Jordan III. This pair has inspired numerous rappers to design their own models. This was the case for the first Drake PEs and even the first Yeezy Nikes, which were inspired by the Tinker Hatfield Jordan IIIs. The Jordan III "Legends of Summer" F&F is also an iconic shoe.

DJ Khaled × Air Jordan III Retro "Grateful" F&F

This was the first pair from the famous DJ and producer to arrive in quantity—and backed by a pretty big marketing strategy, as always. A lucky few among those who preordered the album *Grateful* were selected at random and received this grail shoe. We don't know exactly how many were produced, but I suspect the number was very limited.

DJ Khaled × Air Jordan III Retro "Grateful" F&F

Release date: 06/23/2017
Retail price: Grateful raffle
Resale price: $7,000–$15,000 as of June 2023

DJ Khaled × Air Jordan III "Father of Asahd" F&F

Release date: 09/24/2018
Retail price: pair not sold
Resale price: $6,500–$21,600 (€6,000–€20,000) as of 2023

DJ Khaled × Air Jordan III "Father of Asahd" F&F

There are three pairs of Air Jordan III exclusives specific to DJ Khaled, all just as nice, rare, and expensive as the rest: "Grateful," "Another One," and "Father of Asahd." I've chosen to provide further details about this last pair because they're my favorite. The shoe accompanied the release of the album *Father of Asahd*. The sneakers were originally reserved for DJ Khaled's entourage, but they were also distributed to a few lucky people during a random drawing to promote his album.

WE THE BEST

We The Best × Air Jordan V Retro

Pictured above are the DJ's first two accessible sneaker models, the Sail and the Crimson Bliss, which were released in bigger quantities. The photo also shows two other colors, pink and mint, which were samples—PEs or F&Fs.

We The Best × Air Jordan V Retro
Court Purple F&F (23 pairs)
Polar F&F (23 pairs)
Crimson Bliss
Sail
Release date: 11/28/2022
Retail price: $225
Resale:
Polar F&F model: $3,200 (€3,000) as of June 2023
Court Purple F&F model: $3,200–$6,500 (€3,000–€6,000) as of June 2023
Crimson Bliss and Sail models: under retail

"LEGENDS OF SUMMER," THE PAIR FROM THE TOUR

Air Jordan III Retro "Legends of Summer" F&F

"Legends of Summer" was the name of rapper Jay-Z and singer Justin Timberlake's concert tour. For this 2013 tour, the two artists (and all their musicians) wore this pair. The sneakers were made for the occasion, which makes them all the more exceptional today.

Air Jordan III Retro "Legends of Summer" F&F
Release date: 09/01/2013
Retail price: pair not sold
Resale price: prices at the discretion of the seller and buyer, provided you can find a pair for sale

EMINEM AND JORDAN BRAND

Eminem × Air Jordan IV Retro "Encore" F&F

The story between Eminem and Jordan Brand began in 2003 with a Nike Air Burst "Air Slim Shady" in the Artist Series program, which was released with Pharrell Williams's Dunk High. In 2004, to celebrate Eminem's Encore album, Nike collaborated with the rapper to create three versions of the Air Force 1: two "Shady Records" models—one in white and one in black and white—followed by an "Encore" model in black and white. The latter was exclusively distributed to the artist's friends and family.

Still for the release of his album Encore, rumor had it that Eminem supposedly received fifty pairs of Jordan IV "Encores," which were reserved for Shady Records artists. This model is not stamped "Eminem," but it does incorporate the colors of the album sleeve. In 2021, a Jordan IV "Encore," accompanied by a Shady Records letter signed by Eminem, was sold for $44,100 at Sotheby's.

Eminem × Air Jordan IV Retro "Encore" F&F
Release date: 2005 Retail price: pair not sold Resale price: $16,200–$43,200 (€15,000–€40,000) as of June 2023

In 2006, there were eight series of eight ultra-limited models—fewer than ten pairs each—at Nike, the "Charity Series," which were sold at auction to benefit the Marshall Mathers Foundation founded by Eminem:

1. Eminem × Nike Air Max 1 Charity Series "Big Proof" (tribute to the late rapper Proof from D12)

2. Eminem × Nike Air Max 90 Charity Series "Eminem"

3. Eminem × Nike Air Max 93 Charity Series "D12"

4. Eminem × Nike Air Max 180 Charity Series "Shade 45"

5. Eminem × Nike Air Max 95 Charity Series "Goliath"

6. Eminem × Nike Air Max 97 Charity Series "Shady Records"

7. Eminem × Nike Air Max 360 Charity Series "Inter -scope Records"

8. Eminem × Nike Air Max 2003 Charity Series "Eminem"

Eminem × Air Jordan II Retro "The Way I Am"

This pair accompanied the release of the hip-hop superstar's book The Way I Am. The sneakers feature texts handwritten by the rapper printed on the heel and mudguard. This model was released worldwide as a limited edition of 313 pairs. The number 313 was not chosen at random: It pays tribute to the rapper's hometown of Detroit (313 is its area code). Each of the 313 pairs came with a T-shirt.

Eminem × Air Jordan II Retro "The Way I Am"

Release date: 12/18/2008
Retail price: $110
Resale price: prices at the discretion of the seller and buyer, but often ranging from $4,860 to $8,640 (€4,500–€8,000) as of 2023

Eminem × Air Jordan IV Retro "Encore" F&F

In celebration of the debut of Eminem's album Revival in 2017, the Jordan Brand rereleased this absolute grail shoe from 2005. It's a bit lighter in terms of colors, and I personally prefer this model over the original. As an aside, the latter was manufactured using the same mold as the 2005 shoe.

In 2021, the famous auction house Sotheby's sold two pairs of this rerelease for $50,400 and $56,700.

Eminem × Carhartt WIP × Air Jordan IV Retro

Release date: 11/23/2015
Retail price: pair sold at auction
Resale price: $10,800–$27,000 (€10,000–€25,000) as of 2023

Eminem × Carhartt WIP × Air Jordan IV Retro

Here's the third collaboration between rapper Eminem and Jordan Brand, still with the goal of collecting funds for his charity, the Marshall Mathers Foundation, which helps Detroit youths. Note that these are not the first collaborations between Eminem and Nike—there was a previous, magnificent Nike Air Max 93 "Eminem" in 2006 (just nine pairs were produced). Ten pairs of this model were sold at auction, at prices ranging from $18,000 to $30,000, which brought in a total of $250,000 to the foundation. There was also an F&F pair that was distributed in very small numbers to the superstar's entourage and was also noteworthy due to the contribution from Carhartt, a brand originally from Detroit. This gives even more meaning to this pair, which is full of details, such as the famous backward-facing "E" of Eminem or the equally famous hockey mask on the heels.

Eminem × Air Jordan IV Retro "Encore" F&F

Release date: pair rereleased in 2017
Retail price: pair not sold
Resale price: $48,600–$59,400 (€45,000–€55,000) as of June 2023

KENDRICK LAMAR, FROM REEBOK TO NIKE

For the talented rapper from Compton, Kendrick Lamar, it all began at Reebok in 2015, with one of my favorite models from the brand, the Ventilator. As was often the case with his initial collaborations with Reebok, there's a red pair and a blue pair—corresponding to the Bloods and the Crips gangs. Kendrick Lamar, through his music, his messaging, and collaborations like this one, strongly contributed to establishing a degree of calm in the relations between these two long-standing gangs, which had been rivals forever. The message was clear: Whether red or blue, we were all Black, and, ultimately, we were hurting each other. Here are all the Kendrick Lamar collaborations, with details on the pairs that struck me the most, although for those playing the sneaker game, they are not necessarily all "heats"—in any case, not for the moment!

Kendrick Lamar × Reebok Ventilator "Red and Blue"

The first collaboration between Kendrick Lamar and Reebok was also an occasion to celebrate the twenty-fifth anniversary of the Reebok Ventilator. The rapper insisted on the colors blue and red to symbolize unity between the Bloods and the Crips, rival gangs on the West Coast of the United States. Beneath the tongue is the word "neutral." The insoles contain the inscriptions "Reebok," "Kendrick Lamar," and "TDE," which stands for his label, Top Dawg Entertainment. This pair is one of the most sought-after collaborations between Kendrick Lamar and Reebok and, in my opinion, without a doubt the best executed, although I am aware that I'm biased due to my fondness for the Ventilator!

> **Kendrick Lamar × Reebok Ventilator "Red and Blue"**
> Release date: 07/18/2015
> Retail price: $130
> Resale price: $270–$760 (€250-€700) as of June 2023

January 2016: Kendrick Lamar × Reebok Classic Leather "Red and Blue"

July 2016: Kendrick Lamar × Reebok Classic Leather "Deconstructed"

Kendrick Lamar × Reebok Classic Leather "Perfect Split" Pack (five pairs)

November 2016: Kendrick Lamar × Reebok Classic Leather LUX Olive "Red and Blue"

January 2017: Kendrick Lamar × Reebok Club C "Acid Wash"

In 2017, Kendrick Lamar left Reebok to become a "Nike Family Member." That year was marked by his album Damn, which shattered records: It was the number one album on the Billboard Year-End list, and it won five Grammy Awards and even a Pulitzer Prize, the first time a rapper received that honor. We'd have to wait until January 2018 to see the first pair done in collaboration with Nike. It was obviously a Nike Cortez—it's the iconic shoe of the city of Los Angeles and Compton, and it's also the artist's favorite sneaker, which he'd moreover praised in Big Sean's song Control in 2013.

Kendrick Lamar × Nike Cortez "Kenny 1"

Stamped with a big "DAMN." in place of the traditional Swoosh (in reference to Kendrick Lamar's album), this pair came out the day of the Grammy Awards to celebrate the artist, who won every prize in the rap category. It was nicknamed the "Kenny 1" in reference to one of the artist's nicknames: "Kung Fu Kenny." The legendary Cortez has an incredible history, but it's also a really comfortable pair of shoes. I recommend you buy one half size up, due to its shape.

Kendrick Lamar × Nike Cortez "Kenny 2"

This collaboration was bigger than the first one in terms of demand. That may seem a little strange, but, in this case, it was pretty normal because it's the pair from the photo that Kendrick leaked on his Instagram account in December 2017 and was therefore the most anticipated shoe of his first collaboration with Nike. It was incidentally nicknamed the "Kung Fu Kenny," one of the artist's nicknames, as I mentioned, but also in reference to the Chinese translations around the outer edge of the toe box, which translated to *Damn*, the title of Kendrick Lamar's album. The lace holes are covered with a band that extends onto the heel, which has the words "Don't Trip" embroidered on it.

Kendrick Lamar × Nike Cortez "Kenny 1"
Release date: 01/26/2018
Retail price: $100
Resale price: $216–$650 (€200–€600) as of June 2023

Kendrick Lamar × Nike Cortez "Kenny 2"
Release date: 02/27/2018
Retail price: $100
Resale price: $540–$1,500 (€500–€1,400) as of June 2023

Kendrick Lamar went on to collaborate with Nike on several models:

June 2018: Kendrick Lamar × Nike Cortez "Kenny 3" TDE The Championship

September 2018: Kendrick Lamar × Nike Cortez "Kenny 4" House Shoe

October 2018: Kendrick Lamar × Nike Cortez "Kenny 5" House Shoe

November 2019: Kendrick Lamar × Nike React Element 55

Kendrick Lamar × Nike Cortez "Ale Brown" Sample

No new pairs were due before May 2022, when Kendrick Lamar was set to collaborate with Converse (which Nike owns) through the label PGLang, a communications and entertainment company Kendrick Lamar and Dave Free founded in 2020.

May 2022: PGLang × Converse Chuck Taylor 70 Hi & Pro Leather

THE CENTER OF THE BIGGEST CEREMONIES

Roc-A-Fella × Nike Air Force 1 Low

It would be impossible for me not to mention the AF1 Roc-A-Fella in a section on sneakers and rap. The history between the legendary label, founded by Damon Dash, Shawn Carter (Jay-Z), and Kareem "Biggs" Burke, and Nike began in 2000, when the brand sent Roc-A-Fella Full White F&F sneakers, with the label's logo on the heel, to the teams working there. The shoe is a huge point of pride for people from Harlem, one of the areas in New York to which the AF1s owe their icon status among sneakerheads. In 2003, Jay-Z released *The Black Album* and likewise received the black F&F version of the pair.

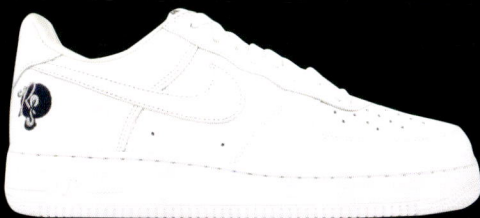

Roc-A-Fella × Nike Air Force 1 Low

Release date: 2004 + rerelease 11/30/2017
Retail price: $90 (2004), $150 (2017)
Resale price:
2004 model: hard to estimate because as of June 2023 it was very rare to find a pair in good condition
2017 model: $216–$490 (€200–€450) as of June 2023

The first official release of the Nike Air Force 1 in collaboration with Roc-A-Fella was in 2004. The event took place in the streets of New York City. The pair was then rereleased in large quantity for a world release in 2017, celebrating the thirty-fifth anniversary of the pair, which was designed by Bruce Kilgore. You can, of course, also find some rare samples, as with many of the major collaborations. That's also the case for collaborations between Roc-A-Fella and other brands, such as Adidas in 2005, or for collaborations between Jay-Z and other brands, such as Puma, for example.

Nike Air Force 1 Low "Questlove"

Release date: 08/16/2008
Retail price: $235
Resale price: $975–$1,300 (€900–€1,200) as of 2023

Jay-Z × Nike Air Force 1 Low "The Black Album" F&F

This pair was produced in very small quantities, for the 2003 release of *The Black Album*. The heel also contains the words "The Black Album," along with the logo of the legendary Def Jam–owned label, Roc-A-Fella Records.

Jay-Z × Nike Air Force 1 Low "The Black Album" F&F

Release date: 12/01/2003
Retail price: pair not sold
Resale price: varies too much to give an average price but ranges between $1,080 and $4,320 (€1,000–€4,000) or even more if the pair is sold at auction

Nike Air Force 1 Low "Questlove"

This is a very limited edition, which was released only in certain Tier 0* stores in the United States. This pair was made in collaboration with the legendary drummer Questlove of the band the Roots. It contains the drummer's silhouette, complete with his Afro cut—which is almost as famous as he is—on the heel.

*Tier Zero (or Tier 0): A Nike account assigned to a boutique. Tier Zero is the best account possible. Nike sends the most limited pairs to Tier Zero stores. In France, you can count the number of Tier 0 stores on one hand. There are several kinds of Tier Zeros—the Tier Zero Jordan, for example.

Nike Air Force 1 BET Hip-Hop Awards 2008 F&F

Only 250 pairs were distributed to artists who did the 2008 BET Awards show. The pair contains the BET logo on the heel and "2008" on the tongue. This pair is just amazing!

Nike Air Force 1 BET Hip-Hop Awards 2008 F&F

Release date: 06/24/2008
Retail price: pair not sold
Resale price: unable to be found

FAT JOE AND TERROR SQUAD

Terror Squad × Nike Air Force 1 Low F&F

Terror Squad is the group that Fat Joe founded in 1998, initially with his best friend, the late Big Pun, but also (among others) Macho, Cuban Link, Triple Seis, and later joined by Remy Ma. It's also the name of the label that Fat Joe created under Atlantic Records in 1999. In 2003, Nike and Fat Joe collaborated on the design of Friends and Family Terror Squad sneakers—the selection process naturally led to the New York sneaker par excellence—the Nike Air Force 1 Low, which is very popular in the Bronx and the Latino community. From 2003 to 2005, several pairs were sent to Terror Squad members. In 2002, one lot of these sneakers ended up at Sotheby's, which upset Fat Joe, who did not appreciate a disgruntled former member putting his pairs up for sale. The white version was designed on the basis of the classic Air Force 1 Lows, with the addition of the logo TS (Terror Squad) on the heel and the words "Don Cartagena" inside, referring to Fat Joe's nickname, which was also the title of his third studio album.

To conclude this "rappers and sneakers" section, I'm going to stay with the Air Force 1s, but in connection to someone I really like on a personal level, both for his music and for his charisma and sense of humor. Naturally, I want to talk about Bronx rapper Joseph Antonio Cartagena, a.k.a. Fat Joe or Joe Crack. Thanks to him, I became aware of my sneaker addiction, after seeing him on an episode of *MTV Cribs* in around 2005, licking the sole of a Jordan 7 Barcelona Olympic in the middle of his enormous collection! It's also thanks to that video, which became a cult favorite, that I decided to start my YouTube channel on sneakers in 2013. I thought it would be cool to talk about a passion that was (at the time) as unique as sneakers, especially since no one was doing that in France.

Terror Squad × Nike Air Force 1 Low F&F

Release date: 2003
Retail price: pair not sold
Resale price: $3,528 at Sotheby's in 2021

Terror Squad × Nike Air Force 1 Low "Macho" Sample

This unique model was made for Fat Joe's best friends from the "Macho" era in 2005.

The shoe was sold at Sotheby's for $4,500. The word "Macho" appears on the heel.

In November 2022, in the show *Full Size Run* on Sole Collector's YouTube channel, Fat Joe makes an appearance wearing Terror Squad × Nike Air Force 1 Low Black Whites—but they're a new pair of sneakers. . . . In the interview, Fat Joe confides that before his death, Virgil Abloh had planned to release Terror Squad × Off-White × Nike Air Force 1 collaborations. Yet another project melding cultural roots with modern fashion that I would have loved to see take shape! Fat Joe explained that he and Nike later worked to make the project a reality and produce Nike Air Force 1 Terror Squads. As of June 2023, the TS × Nike AF1s had not yet been released; however, the official photos of the Nike Black/White turned up, with one difference from the 2004 F&F pair. The most recent shoe has the letters DC (for Don Cartagena) embroidered on the heel. In late 2022, Fat Joe turned up with new TS × Nike Air Force 1s in the same colors as the 2005 "Macho," except that this new pair also had the letters DC on the heel. The rapper confirmed that several colorways from the F&F models would be produced in 2023. Stay tuned . . .

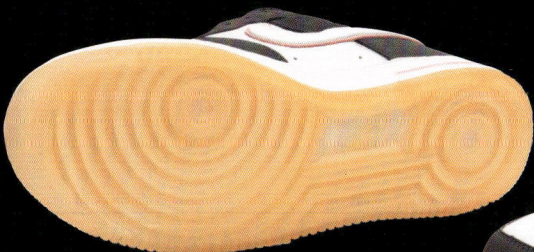

ACKNOWLEDGMENTS

A big thank-you to everyone who agreed to participate in this project!

A special thank-you to @Sneakerdenn, @Toxishoes87, and @_120_kil, and to Charles Michalet for the cover photo.

I thank Julien (JUSBQ#), @kicksssssss, Elie Costa, Rodolphe Muller, brothers Texaco and Teki Latex, Thierry Tek, @Laguezz, Peter Kovkou Kovac and Johanna Kučerovà (Footshop), Ouss, Davassy, Dirty Swift, the Opium Paris team, Moun and Yace, Pierre (@Only_wann), @marionpocasneakers, @Chris.torreto, Larry Deadstock, Bisso (@bisso97120), Christopher (@theworldonthefeet), Kickit Market, Matson (@Epokone_artiste), Pyro, the man in the shadows Joe Gillian, @furio.sab, @margaux_paineau, @empress.cycy, and all the bars of Carreau du Temple, Tiquetonne, and Saint-Sauveur. I'm thinking of all those people (you know who you are!) who have crossed my path at one time or another. I'm so lucky—thank you.

Thanks to my family: Sandrine and Aaliyah, my mother, my father, my sisters, and my French Dutch family.

And thank you to Larousse and the team, who worked so hard, as always, on this beautiful project.

PHOTO CREDITS

Cover

© Charles Michalet

Masthead

© laguezz (p. 5)

Contents

© laguezz (p. 6)

Introduction

© laguezz (p. 8)

Record-Breaking Sneakers

© Kena Betancur/AFP (p. 10)

The Oldest Sneakers in the World!

© Spalding (p. 12), Collection of the Bata Shoe Museum. Image © 2023 Bata Shoe Museum, Toronto, Canada (p. 13)

Record-Setting Sales

© Adidas (p. 14), © Converse (p. 15)

Golden Sneakers!

© Sipa USA/Alamy Live News (p. 16), © PCN Photography / Alamy (p. 17 *top*), © Shutterstock/ Itummy (p. 17 *bottom*), © Nike (pp. 18, 21 *top*, 23), © Sneakers Museum (pp. 19 *top*, 21 *bottom*), © Timothy A. Clary / AFP (pp. 19 *bottom*, 20), © Handout/Sotheby's/AFP (p. 22 *top*), © Christie's Images / BridgemanImages (p. 22 *bottom*)

Sold!

© Kena Betancur / AFP (p. 24 *left*), © GettyImages/ Estrop (p. 24 *right*), © Nike (p. 25), © BISSO97120 (p. 26), © Ed Jones/AFP (p. 27)

Michael Jordan, King of Sneakers

© Nike (p. 28), © Shutterstock / Everett Collection (p. 29)

Sneakers on the Big Screen

© Everett Collection / Bridgeman Images (p. 30)

Now Showing

© Nike (pp. 32 *top left*, 33 *top left*), © Neil Leifer All Rights Reserved (p. 32 *bottom left*), © BISSO97120 (p. 32 *top right*), © Touchstone Pictures / 40 Acres & A Mule Filmworks / Maximum Film / Alamy (p. 33 *top right*), © Buena Vista Pictures / Landmark Media / Alamy (p. 33 *middle*), © Warner Bros Pictures / Landmark Media / Alamy (p. 33 *bottom*), © Warner Bros Pictures / RGR Collection / Alamy (p. 34 *top*), © MGM/UA / Landmark Media / Alamy (p. 34 *bottom*), © Paramount Pictures / PictureLux / The Hollywood Archive / Alamy (p. 35 *left*), © New Balance (p. 35 *right*), © Paramount Pictures / RGR Collection / Alamy (p. 36 *top left*), © Reebok (p. 36 *bottom left*), © Vans (p. 36 *top right*), © Universal Pictures / PictureLux / The Hollywood Archive / Alamy (p. 36 *bottom right*), © Mary Evans / Studiocanal Films Ltd / Alamy (p. 37 *top left*), © Asics (p. 37 *top right*), © Miramax Films / Moviestore Collection Ltd / Alamy (p. 37 *bottom*)

Scene-Stealing Pairs

© Paramount Pictures / Maximum Film / Alamy (p. 38 *top left*), © Shutterstock/2p2play (p. 38 *bottom left*), © Paramount Pictures / AJ Pics / Alamy (p. 38 *right*), © Nike (p. 39 *left*, p. 39 *bottom right*), © Bridgeman Images (p. 39 *top*), © Universal Pictures / Everett Collection / Bridgeman Images (pp. 39 *upper middle*, 39 *lower middle*), © Charles Michalet (pp. 40, 41 *middle*), © Warner Bros Pictures / BFA / Alamy (p. 41 *top*), © Warner Bros Pictures / PictureLux / The Hollywood Archive / Alamy (p. 41 *bottom*), © BISSO97120 (p. 42 *top*), © Thierry Tek (p. 42 *bottom*), © Universal Pictures / PictureLux / The Hollywood Archive / Alamy (p. 43 *top*), © Universal Pictures / Moviestore Collection Ltd / Alamy (p. 43 *bottom*)

A Tribute to the Cinema

© Reebok (pp. 44, 46 *middle*, 46 *bottom*, 47 *top*, 47 *middle*, 51, 52 *bottom*, 53 top, 53 *middle*), © Disney / Pictorial Press Ltd / Alamy (p. 45), © Disney / Entertainment Pictures / Alamy (p. 46 *top*), © Universal Pictures / Pictorial Press Ltd / Alamy (p. 47 *bottom*), © Hughes Entertainment / 20th Century Fox / BFA / Alamy (pp. 48 *top right*, 49 *bottom*), © Adidas (pp. 48 *bottom*, 49 *top*, 49 *middle*, 50 *bottom right*), © Amblin Entertainment / Allstar Picture Library Ltd / Alamy (p. 50 *bottom left*), © Amblin Entertainment / SilverScreen / Alamy (p. 50 *top right*), © 20th Century Fox / Landmark Media / Alamy (pp. 52 *top*, 53 *bottom*)

Alain Gil Gonsalez / Abacapress / Alamy (p. 109 *bottom right*), © Reebok (pp. 110, 111 *middle*, 111 *bottom*, 112 *bottom left*), © Shutterstock / Jonathan Feinstein (p. 111 *top left*), © Shutterstock / Debby Wong (p. 112 *right*)

Adidas Changes the Game

© Shutterstock / Anthony Mooney (p. 114), © sneakerdenn (pp. 115–117), © BAPE (pp. 118 *top*, 121, 122 *bottom*), © Timberland (p. 118 *middle*, 118 *bottom*), © Adidas (pp. 119, 120 *top*, 120 *bottom*, 126, 127 *top right*, 127 *bottom left*, 128 *top left*, 129 *bottom right*, 130 *middle right*, 130 *bottom right*), © Charles Michalet (p. 120 *middle*, 125 *bottom left*, 127 *middle right*, 128 *top right*, 128 *bottom left*, 128 *bottom right*, 129 *top left*, 129 *top right*), © Shutterstock / Carl Bjorklund (p. *122 top left*), © Nike (pp. 122 *middle*, 123 *middle*, 123 *bottom*, 125 *middle left*), © Reebok (p. 123 *top*), © Louis Vuitton (pp. 124, 125 *top right*), © Shutterstock/Ninepal (p. 125 *bottom right*), © Shutterstock / MPH Photos (p. 130 *top*)

Nike's Top Collabs

© Nasser Berzane / Abacapress.com / Alamy (p. 131 *top*), © _120_kil (p. 131 *bottom*), © Nike (pp. 132, 133 *middle*, 133 *bottom*, 134 *top left*, 134 *middle right*, 134 *bottom right*, 135–37, 138 *top right*, 138 *bottom right*, 140 *middle*, 140 *bottom*, 141 *top right*, 141 *bottom right*, 142, 143, 144 *top right*, 145 *middle right*, 145 *bottom left*, 146, 147 *top right*, 148, 149 *bottom right*, 150, 151 *top left*, 151 *top right*, 152 *top right*, 152 *bottom right*, 153), © Shutterstock / Christian Bertrand (pp. 133 *top right*, 149 *bottom left*), © Charles Michalet (p. 134 *top right*, 134 *middle left*, 134 *bottom left*, 139 *middle right*, 139 *bottom right*, 141 *bottom left*, 151 *bottom right*), © Shutterstock/stedalle (p. 138 *left*), © Shutterstock/hurricanehank (p. 139 *bottom left*), © The Canadian Press / Alamy Live News (p. 140 *top right*), © Gonzales Photo / Alamy (p. 144 *bottom left*), © sneakerdenn (p. 144 *lower middle*), © Shutterstock / Kathy Hutchins (pp. 145 *top left*, 147 *top*), © Paul Froggatt / Alamy (p. 152 *middle right*)

Acknowledgments

© laguezz (p. 155)